Multivariate
Taxometric
Procedures

Advanced Quantitative Techniques
in the Social Sciences

VOLUMES IN THE SERIES

Introduction to the Series:
Advanced Quantitative Techniques
in the Social Sciences

The volumes in the new AQTSS series consider quantitative techniques that have proven to be or that promise to be particularly useful for application in the social sciences. In many cases, these techniques will be advanced, not necessarily because they require complicated mathematics, but because they build on more elementary techniques such as regression or descriptive statistics. As a consequence, we expect our readers to have a more thorough knowledge of modern statistics than is required for the volumes in the QASS series. The AQTSS series is aimed at graduate students in quantitative methods specializations, at statisticians with social science interests, and at quantitative social scientists who want to be informed about modern developments in data analysis.

The AQTSS series aims to be interdisciplinary. We prefer to publish volumes about techniques that can be used, and have been used, in different social disciplines and, in some cases, in the behavioral, medical, or physical sciences. This also is reflected in the composition of our editorial board. The board consists of scientists from many different disciplines, all of whom are involved in creating the Department of Statistics at UCLA.

The series also seeks to be practical. Although a good mathematical background may be essential to understand some aspects of the techniques, we insist on an emphasis on real data, real social science problems, and real analyses. This means that both data structures and computer packages get a great deal of emphasis in the volumes of this series.

Statistics present us with a series of techniques that transform raw data into a form that is easier to understand and to communicate or, to put it differently, that make it easy for the data to tell their story. In order to use the results of a statistical analysis in a responsible way, it is necessary to understand the implementations and the sensitivities of the transformations that are applied. We hope that the volumes in this new series contribute to quantitative social science application that are both persuasive and precise.

Jan de Leeuw, UCLA
Richard Berk, UCLA

For information:

SAGE Publications, Inc.
2455 Teller Road
Thousand Oaks, California 91320
E-mail: order@sagepub.com

SAGE Publications Ltd.
6 Bonhill Street
London EC2A 4PU
United Kingdom

SAGE Publications India Pvt. Ltd.
M-32 Market
Greater Kailash I
New Delhi 110 048 India

Printed in the United States of America

Library of Congress Cataloging-in-Publication Data

Waller, Niels G.
    Multivariate taxometric procedures: Distinguishing types from continua /Niels G. Waller, Paul E. Meehl.
        p.   cm. — (Advanced quantitative techniques in the social sciences; 9)
    Includes bibliographical references and index.
    ISBN 0-7619-0257-0 (hardcover: alk. paper)
    1. Psychometrics.   I. Meehl, Paul E. (Paul Everett), 1920-
II. Title.   III. Series.
BF39.W33   1998
150'.1'2—dc21   97-33826

98 99 00 01 02 03 10 9 8 7 6 5 4 3 2 1

This book is printed on acid-free paper.

Acquiring Editor:	C. Deborah Laughton
Editorial Assistant:	Eileen Carr
Production Editor:	Astrid Virding
Production Assistant:	Karen Wiley
Copy Editor:	Joyce Kuhn
Typesetter/Designer:	Janelle LeMaster
Print Buyer:	Anna Chin

Multivariate Taxometric Procedures

Distinguishing Types From Continua

Niels G. Waller

Paul E. Meehl

Advanced Quantitative Techniques
in the Social Sciences Series **9**

SAGE Publications
International Educational and Professional Publisher
Thousand Oaks London New Delhi

For Caprice and Leslie,
two women in a class unto themselves

Contents

Series Editor's Introduction

The book by Waller and Meehl is quite different from previous volumes in the series. On the one hand, it is strongly grounded in classical psychometrics, and its main historical points of reference are the works of Thurstone, Stephenson, Burt, and Cattell. On the other hand, the major field of application of the techniques it describes has been in psychopathology, typically not one of the most quantitative behavioral disciplines. Finally, there is a very strong philosophy of science component in the book, which is used at various points to motivate the developments and to put them in a larger context. All three aspects are quite unique and contribute to making the book, in my view, a very useful addition to the series.

In one important aspect, the Waller and Meehl book resembles the previous volume by Borg and Shye. The extensive work of Guttman on facet analysis was not available in systematic treatment at the graduate level. Borg and Shye provided such a treatment. In the same way, the important and very extensive taxometric work of Meehl was previously available only in articles and reports. This book provides a systematic and carefully written introduction to that work. It also introduces taxometric techniques developed by Waller for multivariate data.

One of the problems with classical psychometrics is that it has been rather insular, perhaps even somewhat inbred. To varying degrees, the same is true for econometrics and sociometrics. One of the explicit purposes of the series is to place the rather specialized techniques developed in these disciplines within the general context of statistics. Yet, as Waller and Meehl repeatedly point out, this will simply not work if statistics are identified with mathematical statistics or inferential statistics. Again, there is a close connection here with the ideas of Louis Guttman. Modern statistics, as I see it, is technique oriented, computational, and thoroughly and completely applied. The Waller and Meehl book indicates this by including S-Plus programs for most of the techniques discussed. This is a very useful feature worthy of repeating in future volumes in the series.

The taxometric work described in this volume seems to have various connections with other areas in modern computational statistics as yet not fully researched. There are various interesting developments in cluster analysis and mixture modeling that could lead to refinements or modifications of the proposed "coherent cut kinetics" techniques. Relations with structural equations modeling and factor analysis, discussed in detail in this book, could perhaps be exploited even further. The all-important fact is that the aims and basic formulation of multivariate taxometrics have now been clearly and distinctly explained.

Knowing which functions are optimized and how the stability of the results is investigated will make it possible for people working in other areas of social and behavioral statistics to relate these technqiues to their own work, and fit them into their frameworks. I hope and expect that this will lead to exciting developments in this unique intersection of cluster analysis and latent variable modeling.

—JAN DE LEEUW
SERIES EDITOR

1

Introduction
Carving Nature at Its Joints

There are two types of people—those who divide the world into types and those who don't.

—Anonymous graffiti,
Tolman Hall, UC Berkeley

Applied scientists are often faced with the difficult task of determining whether data have been sampled from a single population or from a finite set of homogeneous populations; whether observations differ in kind or merely in degree; or whether individual differences arise from types or traits. These questions can sometimes be resolved by using finite mixture models on univariate data (Aitken & Rubin, 1985; Fowlkes, 1979; McLachlan & Basford, 1988; Pearson, 1895; Roeder, 1994), or by applying one or more of the literally hundreds of procedures for classification and clustering that are available for multivariate data (e.g., Blashfield & Aldenderfer, 1988, p. 460, note that there are over 300 varieties of cluster analysis).

The investigator who enters the vast and rapidly expanding classification literature soon discovers that the popularity of the alternatives differs widely among the academic disciplines. Our reading of the literature suggests that statisticians favor parametric mixture models (Lindsay & Basak, 1993; Titterington, Smith, & Makov, 1985); applied psychologists rely (almost exclusively) on cluster analysis algorithms (Everitt, 1993; Fals-Stewart & Lucente, 1993; Haslam & Beck, 1993; Williams, 1994); engineers and neuroscientists prefer neural network models (e.g., unsupervised learning algorithms; Atiya, 1990; Kohonen, 1995; Murtagh, 1995);

and sociologists and psychometricians favor latent class models (Lange-heine & Rost, 1988; Lazarsfeld & Henry, 1968; Rost, 1990, 1991).

Psychiatric nosologists, on the other hand, are increasingly using taxometric procedures (Golden, 1982; Grove & Meehl, 1993; Meehl, 1965, 1973a, 1995a, 1995b; Meehl & Golden, 1982; Meehl & Yonce, 1994, 1996) for distinguishing types[1] (taxa, species, entities, latent classes, natural kinds) from continua (dimensions, latent traits, factors). For example, Meehl's MAXCOV-HITMAX procedure (MAXCOV; Meehl, 1973a; Meehl & Yonce, 1996; see also Grove & Meehl, 1993; Meehl & Yonce, 1994, for related techniques) has recently been used to investigate the latent structure of schizotypy (Korfine & Lenzenweger, 1995; Lenzen-weger & Korfine, 1992; Lowrie & Raulin, 1990); children at risk for schizophrenia (Erlenmeyer-Kimling, Golden, & Cornblatt, 1989); border-line personality disorder (Trull, Widiger, & Guthrie, 1990); psychopathy (Harris, Rice, & Quinsey, 1994); Type A personality (Strube, 1989); and dissociative identity disorder (Waller, Putnam, & Carlson, 1996). In the following chapters we introduce the underlying rationale of MAXCOV and some newly developed multivariate taxometric procedures in simple terms that should be easy to follow without advanced mathematical training.

When writing this book we had three goals in mind. First, we wished to describe MAXCOV (Meehl, 1973a, 1995b; Meehl & Golden, 1982; Meehl & Yonce, 1996) in sufficient detail and clarity so that investigators from a variety of disciplines could profitably use this technique in their taxonomic work. Historically, taxometric studies have been conducted by a small group of psychologists with well-honed programming skills because user-friendly software for taxometric research was not available. To remedy this situation we have written a comprehensive suite of taxometric procedures and utility programs. Copies of these programs are included in the appen-dices of this book. All of our programs are written in S-Plus (StatSci, 1993) because of the superb graphical capabilities and the powerful mathematical routines that are available in this language. The programs are largely self-contained, and hence readers who are not familiar with S-Plus should be able to use the programs with little difficulty.

---

[1] Issues regarding the reality or philosophical status of "taxa," "natural kinds," and "species" have occupied the minds of scientists and natural philosophers for millennia. The term *natural kind* first appears in Mill's (1843) *A System of Logic*. However, the notion of a natural kind can be traced to the works of Plato and Aristotle. For a scholarly discussion of the sometimes protean meanings of these terms in the history of science and taxonomy, see David Hull's (1988) *Science as a Process*.

In line with our second objective, we introduce some recently developed taxometric procedures that allow for the simultaneous analysis of multiple taxon indicators. Two of these procedures, called MAXEIG-HITMAX (MAXEIG) and L-Mode, are discussed in detail and are contrasted with other popular methods for data clustering and classification (e.g., latent profile analysis, Q-technique factor analysis). Third, because both of us are philosophical realists, sticklers for semantic precision, and uncomfortable with the multifarious uses of the terms *taxon* and *type* in the social and biological sciences (see Cattell, 1957, pp. 364-369, for a discussion of 45 meanings of the term *type* in psychology), we devote considerable space to addressing widely held misconceptions concerning the psychometric and philosophical status of taxonic constructs.

We begin our discussion of taxometrics in Chapter 2 by considering several meanings of the term *taxon* and by discussing the philosophy of science that has guided our work in this area. Chapter 3 gets down to basics and offers a detailed account of the General Covariance Mixture Theorem, an equation that undergirds our taxometric procedures. In this chapter, we introduce MAXCOV-HITMAX (Meehl, 1973a; Meehl & Yonce, 1996) and demonstrate how MAXCOV uses the General Covariance Mixture Theorem to test taxonic hypotheses. To facilitate a practical understanding of MAXCOV, we illustrate the procedure with taxometric routines that are included in the appendices of this book. A newly developed taxometric procedure, which we call MAXEIG-HITMAX, is introduced in Chapter 4. The take-home message of Chapter 4 is that MAXEIG is the logical multivariate extension of MAXCOV. In Chapter 5, we introduce a second taxometric newcomer that we call L-Mode. Here you will learn that L-Mode is based on the factor analysis model and that key taxometric parameters can sometimes be estimated with factor analysis. Chapter 6 considers an older factor model for finding groups in data: Q-technique factor analysis (Stephenson, 1936a, 1936b). Our aim in this chapter is to clarify the conditions under which Q-factor analysis and L-Mode yield equivalent results. Finally, in Chapter 7 we provide suggested guidelines for corroborating taxonic models and discuss the role of taxometrics in scientific methodology.

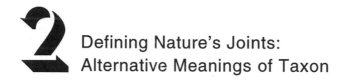

2 Defining Nature's Joints: Alternative Meanings of Taxon

An . . . obvious reason for the collapse of the classical typologies in human personology is the ambiguity of the concept of a type.

—W. G. Dahlstrom (1972, p. 4)

Commonsense Taxa

Three meanings of the methodological term *taxon* are distinguishable, although they are related in a rough empirical way. First, there is a commonsense or standard science usage which does not claim semantic rigor but is satisfactory for many purposes. The familiar words are "species," "syndrome," "disease entity," "type," "category," and "latent class." What they have in common across various disciplines of the life sciences (or even in physics and chemistry, where there are distinct categories such as elementary particles and the various chemical elements) is that they intend to designate a nonarbitrary class, a natural kind, and the user of such a taxonic expression intends to "carve nature at its joints" (Plato). Among accepted taxa that are not in controversy, we have such categories as chipmunks and gophers, igneous and sedimentary rocks, cesium and rubidium, and Trotskyists and Stalinists (for a list of fairly uncontroversial taxa recognized over many disciplines, see Meehl, 1992b). All taxa are classes, but not all classes are taxa (e.g., the size of the class of A students on a final exam might be a function of the instructor's mood while grading the exams). These rough semi-intuitive ways of explaining the term are adequate for many purposes in common life and even in science. But when the existence or the interpretation of a taxon is controversial, as is surely

the case in many fields of the social sciences, or where the whole taxonomic approach is arguable as a research strategy or a clinical practice,
something more rigorous and, unfortunately, also more complicated is
required.

Causal Origin Taxa

A second meaning, often taken as a clarifying explication of the commonsense one, refers to the causal origin of a natural kind or nonarbitrary
class. Thus, some disputes in the taxonomy of plants and animals are
approached from the standpoint of their phyletic origin on the evolutionary
tree. Disease entities in organic medicine are specified jointly by their
pathology and etiology when both are known and by pathology when the
etiology is as yet undiscovered (Meehl, 1973b, pp. 285-287). While it is
natural in the life sciences to think in terms of germs and genes ("the
medical model"), one should not overlook other causal sources that give
rise to strong taxa, such as tightly knit ideologies in political science or
psychopathological syndromes traceable to life history events or regimes.
Thus, for example, some clinicians (Waller, Putnam, & Carlson, 1996)
believe that dissociative identity disorder is a true taxon, a "type" of mental
condition, with a specific etiology consisting of childhood sexual abuse.
There is no metatheoretical basis for assuming that only a disorder produced by a germ or a gene should be thought of as taxonic, whereas
disorders stemming from social-environmental conditions (e.g., having
been sexually abused in childhood) are not real taxa because their etiology
is not biological in the narrow sense of that word. Some of the strongest,
most tightly knit taxa in human behavior are what Cattell (1946) calls
"environmental mold" types (just as there are environmental mold dimensions). The elements of such a syndrome may or may not have some sort
of intrinsic semantic or causal relation pairwise, but the main source of the
nonarbitrary class lies in the social or educational environment (e.g., being
raised in a Baptist family, majoring in chemistry). An individual exposed
to a certain schedule of reinforcements with respect to shaped behavior R_1
will (almost always) have been concurrently exposed to a strong schedule
with respect to behavior R_2. Occupational taxa provide a clear and important example of environmental mold categories; in the *Dictionary of
Occupational Titles* (U.S. Department of Labor, 1977) we find some
20,000 occupational syndromes.
    That there are so many paths to an end state of taxonicity means that the
definition of taxon with reference to etiology will unavoidably be hetero-

geneous. We know of no philosophical or empirical argument showing that, having listed all the kinds of causal influences that can eventuate in nonarbitrary categories, one would be able to discern a common property among these causes. If Freud's original theory of the life history difference in etiology between hysteria and obsessional neurosis (Freud, 1896/1962a, 1896/1962b, 1896/1962c) had been correct, this would have been an example of specific etiology and, despite not being a germ or a gene, would provide a perfectly good basis for the classification in terms of causation (cf. discussion of meanings of "specific etiology" in Meehl, 1977).

Formal-Numerical Taxa

A third meaning, clearer than the first, but more outcome-neutral than the second, is a purely formal-numerical definition. Like multiple-factor analysis, multidimensional scaling, cluster analysis, latent class analysis, and other well-known statistical procedures, it sits loose with respect to causality and focuses on the numerical relations among the various candidate indicators of a conjectured taxon. While empirically based, this approach is substantively neutral. It is important to remember that no statistical procedure is ever self-interpreting, even the simplest, such as significance tests and correlation coefficients (Bolles, 1962; Meehl, 1978). This methodological truism is the best answer to those concerned about the danger of "discovering" spurious taxa, categories that do not carve nature or society at its joints but are consequences of some institutional process, such as an administrative decision (see Grayson, 1987). One who identifies a statistical taxon by a trustworthy taxometric method is under the same obligation as any scientist (or, for that matter, any rational person!) to follow the logician's total evidence rule (Carnap, 1950/1962, sec. 45b; Salmon, 1984). In doing this, one must make a crucial distinction, routinely ignored in statistics texts, between the scientific appraisal of a substantive (causal or compositional) theory and the statistical inference on which this appraisal is based. Conventional instruction in inferential statistics misleads many students into thinking that the big problem in research is presented by the transition from a statistic to a parameter and that one must therefore turn to the statistician for the answers to difficult methodological questions about the appraisal of substantive scientific theories. This is erroneous, as is easily seen by asking a simple question from one of our own areas of research: "Suppose we had the exact value of the parameter, say the proportion of siblings of schizophrenic probands who showed a particular neurological anomaly; how confident should we be of a dominant gene theory of schizotaxia?" There is no algorithm for quantifying the confirmation or corroboration of substantive scientific theories, given a collection of quantitative values assumed to be statistically trustworthy, and most logicians doubt that any such number-generating machinery of "inductive logic" is even possible. Even should they be mistaken about that, it is clear that nobody claims to have one at the present time that is usable by the working scientist in theory appraisal. It is controversial whether the logician's and epistemologist's (and lawyer's) meaning of the term *probability* is always susceptible of numerification. The Bayesians attempt this project by moving from the objective to the subjective and quantifying the latter kind of judgmental probability in terms of what the individual knower would consider fair betting odds on various beliefs (Howson & Urbach, 1993). We do not denigrate objective probability numbers, and in later chapters we make some suggestions about that vexed question, but this will involve important departures from certain features of conventional statistical reasoning in the social sciences (for a detailed discussion of this parameter estimation/theory appraisal problem, see Meehl, 1978, 1990a, 1990e).

Misconceptions and Confusions
About Taxonic Constructs

Bimodality Is Not Required

It is a persistent misconception that an indicator of an underlying taxon must be bimodally distributed. If life were so simple, we would not have to resort to sophisticated mathematical procedures. Bimodality is neither a necessary nor a sufficient condition for latent taxonicity (see, e.g., Grayson, 1987; Murphy, 1964), a point that is easily illustrated. Consider, for example, the situation depicted in Figure 2.1. This figure portrays composite and component frequency distributions for a mixture (base rate equals one-half) of two latent (normal) distributions of equal variance and a mean difference of two standard deviations. Notice that the smoothed composite distribution is unimodal; that is, there are no obvious discontinuities in the observed scores. "For a fixed mean difference, reduction in the base rate shifts the composite curve from platykurtosis to leptokurtosis with a correlated rise in skewness, a complicated exchange in the manifest distribution that remains to be thoroughly investigated" (Meehl, 1995a, p. 269). Of course, bimodality on real-valued characters is suggestive of taxonicity, and marked platykurtosis or marked skewness may also be.

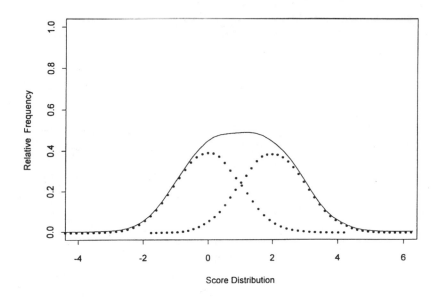

Figure 2.1   Mixture of Two Normal Distributions

Bimodality on total scores from summed dichotomous (e.g., true/false personality items) or otherwise coarsely measured indicators (e.g., 5-point Likert-type items) can also be suggestive of taxonicity, although at other times it reflects an unpropitious conjunction of person and item characteristics.

Taxonicity Is Not "Merely a Moderator Effect"

Another misconception is that what appears to be taxonicity could be "merely a moderator effect." The taxonic curve we obtain with taxometric procedures is *of course* due to a "moderator effect" if that phrase is used in the purely statistical sense, absent any stronger imputations of one or another kind of causality. The original definition of a moderator variable was one that "influences" (in the minimal sense of *statistically* correlates with) the correlation of two others. Hence, the objection "merely" a moderator effect must imply something additional, perhaps that it is a continuous (noncategorical) moderator variable operating as a latent factor, and the criticism then becomes a question about the confidence one can have in the inferred latent structure. An underlying noncategorical causal factor would have to generate a taxonic-looking graph (as described in Chapter 3) by exerting a nonmonotone effect on the output correlation of a sort which has not been discovered, despite many years of work on moderators. It is generally known that moderator effects are very hard to find and, when they do show replicability and validity generalization, are so small in size as to be neither practically important nor theoretically illuminating. It seems unsettled whether, in the small number of sizable, replicable moderator effects, categorical moderators such as gender, race, and social class preponderate (as we suspect they do) over quantitative moderators. Thus, "merely" a moderator effect must be parsed as what kind—quantitative or categorical? By definition, latent taxonicity is a (categorical) moderator effect. The explanation of taxonic results found via procedures such as we describe here is inconsistent with a nontaxonic latent moderator variable.

Taxonicity Does Not Preclude Dimensionality

Inferring that a latent structure is taxonic does not imply that there is no latent dimension involved. In most situations, the existence of taxonicity is an "additional" feature, something along with latent dimensions that in turn "underlie" the manifest dimensions and that produce them. Thus, the convenient dichotomy taxonic-vs.-dimensional should, strictly speaking, read "taxonic-dimensional vs. *dimensional only*." The language "taxonic-vs.-nontaxonic" conveys this adequately, as it carries no implied denial of latent dimensions (quantitative variables, factors). For example, a Mendelizing mental deficiency (e.g., PKU) is a clear genetic taxon. Psychometrically, one understands the phenotypic effects of this mutation to be mediated by an enzyme deficiency which results in serum accumulation of phenylalanine and its metabolites, which in turn impairs brain cell function, which lowers psychometrically measured general intelligence (psychometric g), thereby lowering the set of WISC (a popular intelligence test for children) subtest performances. Psychometric g is a quantitative entity, but the genetic taxon results in its distribution being a mixture case. In that sense, the various search procedures for taxa may all be conceptualized as different ways of detecting admixtures in one or more inferred latent distributions.

Most Taxa Are Initially Specified by Imperfect Indicators

A serious mistake is confusing the underlying taxon with the indicators we use to measure it. The underlying taxon may be more or less sharply defined depending on the causal structure (e.g., having or not having the Huntington mutation versus a socially defined, nonbiological taxon such as childhood trauma) and the level at which we are measuring it (e.g., the Huntington *syndrome* is not sharply defined because, for instance, not all carriers of the genetic mutation live long enough to exhibit the disease). Whether or not an underlying taxon is an all-or-nothing category, the indicators we have available to detect and measure the taxon are rarely perfect, hence the need for sophisticated taxometric procedures. Sometimes the fallibility of the indicators is partly a function of the level at which we are measuring the taxon. In a genetic taxon, for example, many modifiers and potentiators can intervene between the DNA and a behavioral manifestation. Of course, the usual reasons for fallibility of psychometric measures also obtain. It is important not to confuse the underlying structure—taxonic or nontaxonic—with indicator variables— qualitative or quantitative—that may be used to detect that structure. Any combination of these is possible (see Meehl, 1995a, p. 268).

3 Mathematical Foundations of Multivariate Taxometrics

There are gophers, there are chipmunks, but there are no gophmunks.

—Paul Meehl in award acceptance speech to
the American Psychological Association,
August 14, 1994

In Chapter 2, we learned that the term *taxon* has several distinguishable meanings. In this chapter, we focus on one particular meaning that can be formalized by a versatile equation called *the General Covariance Mixture Theorem*. After examining this theorem in its many guises, we describe a powerful technique—called MAXCOV-HITMAX (Meehl, 1965, 1973a, 1995b; Meehl & Golden, 1982; Meehl & Yonce, 1996)—that can be used to estimate its parameters. To breathe life into these equations, in the final section we illustrate an example MAXCOV analysis.

The General Covariance Mixture Theorem

The General Covariance Mixture Theorem was first described by Paul Meehl more than three decades ago (Meehl, 1965, pp. 12, 28-29; see also Meehl, 1968, pp. 4-5) in a widely circulated technical report from the University of Minnesota. In that report, Meehl described a convenient expression for partitioning a mixed-sample covariance into its constituent parts.

Meehl noted that the covariance of a pair of taxon indicators, say, x and y, could be expressed as an estimable linear function of the following terms[1]:

$$cov(xy) = Pcov_t(xy) + Qcov_c(xy) + PQ(\bar{x}_t - \bar{x}_c)(\bar{y}_t - \bar{y}_c), \qquad (3.1)$$

where

$cov(xy)$ is the covariance of x and y in the total (i.e., mixed) sample

P is the base rate of taxon members in the total sample

$Q = 1 - P$ equals the base rate of complement (nontaxon) members in the total sample

$Pcov_t(xy)$ is the weighted indicator covariance in the taxon (t) class

$Qcov_c(xy)$ is the weighted indicator covariance in the complement (c) class

$PQ(\bar{x}_t - \bar{x}_c)(\bar{y}_t - \bar{y}_c)$ is the weighted cross-product of the latent class mean differences

Meehl called this equation the General Covariance Mixture Theorem. Although the original theorem focused on covariances, it is easily shown that the General Covariance Mixture Theorem can also be used to represent other summary statistics in mixed populations. For example, a Pearson product moment correlation (r) is simply a covariance between standardized scores; consequently, the theorem implies that

$$r(xy) = P\frac{cov_t(xy)}{sd(x)sd(y)} + Q\frac{cov_c(xy)}{sd(x)sd(y)} + PQ\frac{(\bar{x}_t - \bar{x}_c)(\bar{y}_t - \bar{y}_c)}{sd(x)sd(y)}. \qquad (3.2)$$

Moreover, the variance of a variable (var) is the covariance of the variable with itself; thus the theorem also implies that

$$var(x) = Pvar(x_t) + Qvar(x_c) + PQ(\bar{x}_t - \bar{x}_c)^2, \qquad (3.3)$$

or in standard score form,

$$var(x_z) = 1.00 = P\frac{var(x_t)}{var(x)} + Q\frac{var(x_c)}{var(x)} + PQ\frac{(\bar{x}_t - \bar{x}_c)^2}{var(x)}. \qquad (3.4)$$

Additional variations of these formulae are possible, but, rather than consider those equations, at this point it may be more helpful to examine the General Covariance Mixture Theorem from a graphical perspective.

Consider the scatterplot in Figure 3.1. This plot was constructed by generating 100 paired observations on two taxon indicators, which for

---

[1] A formal proof of the General Covariance Mixture Theorem appears in Appendix A of Meehl and Yonce (1996).

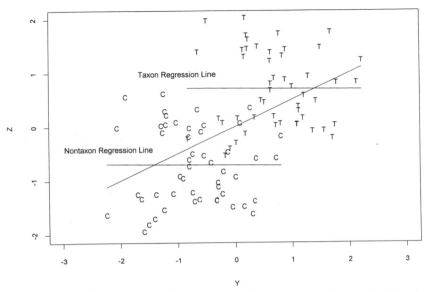

Figure 3.1. Taxon Indicator Regressions in Component and Composite Samples

convenience we call y and z. The observations for y and z were drawn from a two-population mixed distribution; the higher-scoring population represents the taxon class. Taxon members are denoted by a T in the figure, and complement (nontaxon) members are denoted by a C. Each population contains 50 paired observations, so the base rate of the taxon class is .5. The within-class distributions for each variable are approximately normal, with unit standard deviations. For nontaxon members, the indicators are centered at −1.00; for taxon members, they are centered at 1.00. That is, the indicator means are two within-class σ (standard deviation) units apart. It was shown in Chapter 2 that under these conditions the univariate distributions for y and z are *not* likely to exhibit bimodality.

For both the taxon and nontaxon groups, the within-class correlations are precisely zero and the within-class regression lines are correspondingly flat. In the mixed sample, however, y and z correlate appreciably, for reasons described by the General Covariance Mixture Theorem. Specifically, y and z correlate in the mixed sample—even though they do not correlate in the component samples—because their means in the taxon and complement groups differ. The mixed-sample regression line has a positive slope and, accordingly, the mixed-sample correlation is .50. We now demonstrate how to calculate this value from the General Covariance Mixture Theorem.

Recall that Equation (3.3) describes a total-sample variance as a function of (a) the taxon and complement variances, (b) the taxon base rate, and (c) the differences between the latent class indicator means. In the present case, we know the values of these parameters because we generated the data. Plugging these values into Equation (3.3) reveals that

$$var(y) = 2.00 = (.50 \times 1.00) + (.50 \times 1.00) + .25(2.00)^2.$$

The same procedure is used to calculate the variance of z. Having calculated these quantities we are now in a position to calculate the mixed-sample correlation via Equation (3.2). If the math is performed correctly we find that the theoretically implied and the empirically calculated correlations agree perfectly:

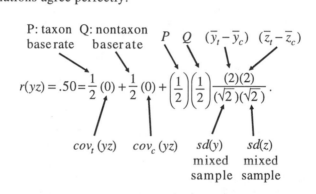

Solving these equations was an instructive exercise, although needless to say, in most taxometric investigations the latent-distribution summary statistics (e.g., the within-class variances, covariances, or means) are unknown. Indeed, in many situations even the taxonic status of the data is unknown. Suppose, however, that for a given data set we have a clinical hunch or a theoretically derived conjecture that the data come from two distinguishable groups. Further suppose that the data are truly taxonic. If this last supposition is correct, taxometric procedures that are founded on the General Covariance Mixture Theorem can be used to (a) empirically partition the indicator distributions into their constituent parts, (b) estimate the taxon base rate, and (c) assign observational units to the taxon or nontaxon groups. For example, when three or more taxon indicators are available, a powerful taxometric procedure called MAXCOV (Meehl, 1973a; Meehl & Golden, 1982; Meehl & Yonce, 1996) can often be used to solve the parameters of the General Covariance Mixture Theorem and to accomplish the aforementioned goals. Before discussing MAXCOV, let us consider an additional variation of this theorem that will help us understand the mathematical underpinnings of our taxometric procedures.

Taxa as Regression Model Dummy Scores

Several years ago, Jacob Cohen (1968; see also Cohen, 1992), in a highly influential paper on data analysis, demonstrated that any analysis of variance (ANOVA) model could be handled by a multiple regression model if the *qualitative* grouping variables were coded as dummy scores (see Aiken & West, 1991, chap. 7, for a thorough discussion of dummy coding). Cohen's observation is relevant here because group membership in taxonic models can be coded as dummy scores in regression models.

To illustrate this point, consider the final term of Equation (3.4):

$$\left(PQ \frac{(\bar{x}_t - \bar{x}_c)^2}{var(x)} \right).$$

Notice here that this fraction denotes the proportion of variance in a mixed sample that can be ascribed to the taxon mixture (i.e., the base rate). Another way of characterizing this term is to recognize that it equals the R^2 (the coefficient of determination) that is obtained when x, a fallible taxon indicator, is regressed on a *dichotomous dummy variable* that signifies taxon membership. Call this dummy variable d and assume, as is customary in one statistical tradition, that the dummy scores take on values of 0 or 1.00. Under these conditions, the expected value of $d = P$, $Q = 1 - P$, and $var(d) = PQ$.

Let r_{xd} represent the correlation between indicator x and the latent class variable, d. Equation (3.4) implies that r_{xd} can be expressed as

$$r_{xd} = \sqrt{\frac{PQ(\bar{x}_t - \bar{x}_c)^2}{var(x)}} = \frac{(PQ)^{\frac{1}{2}}(\bar{x}_t - \bar{x}_c)}{sd(x)} \tag{3.5}$$

Furthermore, the covariance between x and d is

$$cov(xd) = r_{xd} \cdot sd(x) \cdot sd(d) \tag{3.6}$$

$$= (PQ)(\bar{x}_t - \bar{x}_c), \quad \text{because } sd(d) = (PQ)^{1/2}; \tag{3.7}$$

and the regression coefficient of x on d is

$$\beta_{xd} = \frac{cov(xd)}{PQ} = (\bar{x}_t - \bar{x}_c).\qquad(3.8)$$

These equations describe some fundamental properties of two-group mixtures. In this book, we limit our attention to two-group mixture distributions for several reasons. First, two-group mixtures—consisting of a taxon and a complement class—arise commonly in our substantive research areas (psychopathology and behavior genetics). Second, taxometric procedures for three or more groups, from the family of procedures emphasized in this book, have not been sufficiently perfected, although we are currently working on some promising techniques. This does not mean, however, that the General Covariance Mixture Theorem is applicable to two-group problems only. On the contrary, the theorem is perfectly generalizable and can accommodate sampling schemes with any number of latent classes (see Haertel, 1990, especially Equation 12, for further details).

MAXCOV-HITMAX

For over three decades, Paul Meehl has been developing and refining a series of taxometric procedures that are known collectively as the "coherent cut kinetics method" (we describe the defining features of these techniques in the next chapter). Meehl's MAXCOV-HITMAX (Meehl, 1965, 1973a, 1995a, 1995b; Meehl & Golden, 1982; Meehl & Yonce, 1996)—or MAXCOV (MAXimum COVariance)—is the most popular procedure from this class of models (for recent applications, see Strube, 1989; Waller, Putnam, & Carlson, 1996).

In this section, we describe the mathematical foundations of MAXCOV and use the General Covariance Mixture Theorem as our organizational framework. Recall that this important theorem can be expressed as

$$cov(xy) = Pcov_t(xy) + Qcov_c(xy) + PQ(\bar{x}_t - \bar{x}_c)(\bar{y}_t - \bar{y}_c).$$

Notice in this equation that the first two terms will drop out whenever the within-class covariances are zero. Under this condition it is easily proved that a mixed-sample covariance is a simple function of the taxon base rate (P) and the differences between the indicator means in the latent classes. For example, if x and y are uncorrelated in the latent taxa,

$$cov(xy) = PQ(\bar{x}_t - \bar{x}_c)(\bar{y}_t - \bar{y}_c).\qquad(3.9)$$

We use the term *nuisance covariance* to denote the within-class covariation in the complement, the taxon, or both groups. Equation (3.9) implies that when nuisance covariance is zero—that is, when the taxon and complement covariances are zero—the mixed-sample covariance is a simple function of *the profile of indicator means* and the taxon base rate.

Stated formally, Equation (3.1) reduces to Equation (3.9) when nuisance covariance is absent. We emphasize this point because zero nuisance covariance is an auxiliary conjecture of the MAXCOV formalism. In other words, when we derive the MAXCOV equations we assume that nuisance covariance is absent. As a practical stance, however, we realize this auxiliary conjecture is an idealization that will rarely be satisfied in MAXCOV applications. In the social sciences, as David Lykken (1991) has wryly observed, "everything is likely to be related at least a little bit to everything else, for complex and uninteresting reasons" (p. 31). Lykken calls this omnipresent covariation the *crud factor*.

Fortunately, simulation studies suggest that the crud factor only rarely vitiates MAXCOV parameter estimates. For example, Monte Carlo runs that are summarized in Meehl and Golden (1982, Table 5.2, p. 163) indicate that MAXCOV accurately estimates a key taxometric parameter, known as the hitmax point, whenever nuisance *correlations* are less than .50 (an extension of MAXCOV can be used when nuisance correlations are more than .50; see Meehl, 1995b, for details). In the next section, we see why this is such an important finding.

Locating the Hitmax

We use the term *hitmax* to denote the point on a mixed distribution where the ordinates of the latent complement and taxon (unrelativized) density functions intersect. To better understand this concept, consider Figure 3.2, where we have identified the hitmax for the sample distributions that were previously illustrated in Chapter 2. Notice, in this figure, that when individuals with scores greater than the hitmax are classified as taxon members, and all other individuals are classified as nontaxon members, cutting the indicator at the hitmax score produces a greater number of classification "hits" than any other point along the indicator distribution (see Meehl, 1973a, for mathematical details).

MAXCOV can be used to locate the hitmax whenever three conjectured taxon indicators are available and at least one indicator is measured on a continuous scale (or a quasi-continuous scale, such as a 10-point Likert-

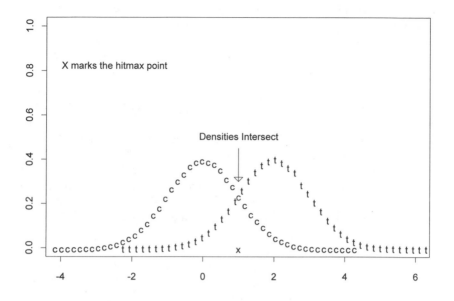

Figure 3.2.   Hitmax Occurs at Intersection of Latent Density Functions

type scale). Ideally, in the taxon and complement groups, the three or more indicators are pairwise uncorrelated (i.e., have zero nuisance covariance) and have means that are widely separated (i.e., have high validity). To best approximate these conditions, we recommend choosing theoretically relevant indicators from different domains (e.g., in the field of psychopathology we might choose taxon indicators from physiological measures, personality scores, and cognitive performance tasks). To illustrate these ideas, let us suppose that we are conducting a MAXCOV analysis with three diverse indicators, which for lack of more imaginative names we call x, y, and z.

Our analysis begins by designating one variable, say x, as the MAXCOV *input* variable, and the remaining variables—in this case, y and z—as the MAXCOV *output* variables. The meanings of these terms will become clear shortly. After designating the input and output indicators, we sort all the variables on the basis of the *ordered* input scores. Next, the sorted *input* scores are divided into a series of contiguous and nonoverlapping subsamples and for each subsample we compute the covariance between the *output* variables, y and z.

Let x_i denote a fixed interval on input variable x, and let $cov_{x_i}(yz)$ denote the conditional covariance between y and z for cases in x_i. We say that the lower and upper boundary points on x_i define a *slab* of x. Equation (3.9) implies that the output covariances for sequential x-slabs will form an orderly pattern if the indicators measure a latent taxon and a different, though predictable, pattern if they measure a latent dimension. For taxon indicators, the covariances vary systematically as a function of the x-slab *taxonic mix* (defined as the proportion of taxon members in the x-slab). Specifically, in successive x-slabs, the output covariances increase from zero to a maximum and then decrease to zero. For dimensional indicators, on the other hand, the output covariances should be relatively constant across the x-slabs (within the limits of sampling error). This suggests that by considering the series of output covariances we can distinguish taxonic from dimensional markers. Let us consider this point further by reviewing the previous steps in greater detail.

As noted beforehand, in the first stage of a MAXCOV analysis the input scores are sorted and partitioned into a series of contiguous x-slabs (subsamples) of constant width. Suppose, for our illustration, we have data on 600 individuals and that the standardized x scores range from -3.00 to $+3.00$. In comparable situations we have found that an x-slab width of 1/4 standard deviation often works well.[2] Because the slab boundaries determine the minimum number of cases in an x-slab, in smallish samples—say, with less than 200 or 300 cases—we might use a slab width of 1/3 or 1/2 standard deviation.

Continuing with our example, for the initial x-slab we identify all cases falling in the interval $-3.00 \leq x < -2.75$, and for these cases—and these cases only—$cov(yz)$ is computed and saved for later analysis. Next, we pull out the x scores falling in the interval $-2.75 \leq x < -2.50$ and compute $cov(yz)$ for this subsample. We repeat this process until all x scores have been exhausted.

	cov_{yz}	cov_{yz}			cov_{yz}
	for cases	for cases			for cases
	in 1st	in 2nd			in last
	x-slab	x-slab			x-slab
input x:					
x-slabs:	1st	2nd		...	last

---

[2] An old (precomputer) convention, attributed to Karl Pearson, said that when grouped data were computationally imperative, class intervals of 1/4 standard deviation were "fine enough," losing only 10% of the available information.

If x is a valid, though fallible indicator of a latent taxon, then sorting y and z on the basis of x also fallibly sorts the indicators on the basis of taxon membership. With even moderate validity, the x-slabs at the lower and upper extremes of the distribution should contain primarily nontaxon and taxon members, respectively. Stated otherwise, the taxon base rate is approximately 0.00 in the lowest x-slab and approximately 1.00 in the highest x-slab. When the sample contains an even mix of taxon and nontaxon members, that is, when the grand taxon base rate is 1/2, an x-slab exists in the middle of the distribution that also contains a 50-50 mix of group members. When $P < 1/2$, this interval is shifted to the right; when $P > 1/2$, it is shifted to the left. Moving away from this interval, the *conditional* taxon rate, p_i, which is defined as the relative proportion of taxon members in an x-slab, decreases as x gets smaller and increases as x gets larger (assuming that taxon members receive higher scores on x). The conditional complement rate, $q_i = 1 - p_i$, behaves oppositely.

Earlier, we noted that at the distribution extremes the x-slabs are composed primarily of taxon ($p_i \approx 1.00$, $q_i \approx 0.00$) or complement ($p_i \approx 0.00$, $q_i \approx 1.00$) members, and in the absence of nuisance covariance, Equation (3.9) predicts that in these regions the expected output covariance of y and z will equal zero (whenever p_i or q_i equals 0.00, the left-hand side of Equation [3.9] also equals 0.00). Moving upward on the x distribution, the output covariances increase until they reach a maximum (peak) in the x-slab with the greatest taxonic mix. This occurs when $p_i \approx q_i \approx .50$ and $p_i q_i \approx .25$.

After this point the conditional taxon and complement rates diverge and the corresponding x-slab covariances decrease. Accordingly, with taxonic data, a plot of the output covariances against the x-slab midpoints resembles a hump or a peak. When the total-sample base rate is 1/2, the peak occurs near the center of the graph. For smaller base rates, the peak shifts to the right; for larger base rates, it shifts to the left. In other words, the shape of the graph of the conditional covariances provides a graphical means of evaluating the taxonic conjecture and of determining the size of the taxon base rate. These concepts are illustrated in Figure 3.3.

Panel A depicts a MAXCOV plot of taxonic data with a base rate of .50. Notice that at the lower end of the sorted input scores the output covariance is approximately zero (because $p_i \approx 0.00$). In higher x-slabs, the output covariances increase until they reach a maximum. The maximum in this plot occurs when $x = .10$. After this point the output covariances decrease and—as predicted by the General Covariance Mixture Theorem—eventually return to zero. Notice that the peak of the function occurs in the vicinity of the hitmax score. For this example, the true hitmax occurs at

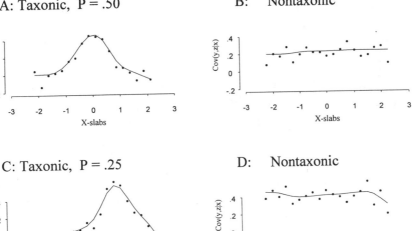

Figure 3.3.   Example MAXCOV-HITMAX Plots for Taxonic and Nontaxonic Data

0.00, whereas the estimated hitmax occurs at .10. Notice, also, that a standard score of .10 demarcates the upper 46% of a (standard) normal distribution and that 46% is close to the taxon base rate (50%). Finally, notice that in this and in later MAXCOV examples we have smoothed the conditional output covariances with a running medians smoother that is attributed to Tukey (4[3RSR]2H *twice*; Tukey, 1977, chaps. 7 & 16). In our experience, this last step generally improves the quality of the hitmax estimates.

Panel B in Figure 3.3 displays a MAXCOV plot of nontaxonic data. The data for this example were drawn from a homogeneous population in which the variables load on a single common factor. That is, we are working with dimensional indicators—there is no taxon—and the MAXCOV plot is appropriately flat. It is worth noting that the *total-sample* correlations for the output variables in Panels A and B are equivalent (*all* indicator correlations in Panels A and B equal 0.50). For these examples we generated data sets with equal correlation matrices to illustrate an important point:

By simply eyeballing a correlation or covariance matrix it is impossible to distinguish taxonic from dimensional data. Many investigators fail to recognize this point and falsely believe that if a data matrix can be approximated by a covariance structure model, such as a confirmatory factor analysis model, then the taxonic hypothesis is necessarily discorroborated (see Bartholomew, 1987, pp. 36-37; Haertel, 1990; Molenaar & Von Eye, 1994, for holes in this logic).

Panel C in Figure 3.3 displays a second taxonic MAXCOV plot. Here, the taxon base rate is .25 and the estimated hitmax is .686. Impressively, the estimated and true hitmax in this example are equal. Furthermore, a standard score of .686 demarcates the upper 25% of a standard normal distribution. Because the base rate in Panel C is smaller than .50, the peak of the MAXCOV function properly occurs to the right of the distribution midpoint. Note that for extreme base rates—say, when the base rate is smaller than .10—the conditional slope (derivative) of a (possibly smoothed) MAXCOV function can fail to change sign. In this case the function's graph will have no peak. This unfortunate situation occurs primarily in small to moderately sized data sets where it is difficult to create *x*-slabs with a preponderance of taxon members. In such instances, the absence of a clear-cut peak should not be taken as evidence against the taxonic conjecture.[3] A flat MAXCOV function that rises precipitously at the upper end of the input distribution *is* consistent with a low-base-rate taxon.

The final panel in Figure 3.3, Panel D, displays a second nontaxonic MAXCOV plot. Notice here that the conditional covariances in Panel D are generally larger than the covariances in Panel B. This occurs because the *dimensional* indicators in the final example (Panel D) are more strongly correlated (i.e., have higher factor loadings) than the indicators in the second example (Panel B).

To summarize the main points of this section, we have learned that, by its overall shape, a MAXCOV plot indicates whether the data measure a latent taxon (type, class) or a latent dimension (continuum, factor). If the possibly smoothed MAXCOV function forms a peak rather than a line, the taxonic hypothesis is corroborated. We have also learned that, by its

---

[3]In instances when the taxon base rate is very small, and when the derivative of the MAXCOV function does not change sign (it increases indefinitely), it may be useful to temporarily discard cases with extremely low input scores and reconduct the MAXCOV analysis. Individuals with very low scores are almost certainly nontaxon members. Consequently, the reduced sample will have a larger base rate.

relative position, the maximum of a MAXCOV plot indicates the approximate value of the sorting indicator (input variable) hitmax score. Moreover, the estimated hitmax score can be used to obtain a preliminary estimate of the taxon base rate. With the methods described below, MAXCOV can produce more accurate estimates of the base rate and other taxonic parameters.

Estimating the Grand Base Rate and Indicator Validities

A key result of the last section is that, in the absence of nuisance covariance, a conditional covariance between taxon indicators can be parsimoniously expressed by the reduced form of the General Covariance Mixture Theorem:

$$cov_i(yz) = p_i q_i (\bar{y}_t - \bar{y}_c)(\bar{z}_t - \bar{z}_c) .$$

Let us examine this equation more closely. In particular, notice that the latent indicator means ($\bar{y}_t, \bar{y}_c, \bar{z}_t,$ and $\bar{z}_c$) do not have a subscript i because they do not change over x-slabs. Accordingly, we can further simplify this equation by letting $\Delta_{\bar{y}} = (\bar{y}_t - \bar{y}_c)$, $\Delta_{\bar{z}} = (\bar{z}_t - \bar{z}_c)$, and $K = \Delta_{\bar{y}} \Delta_{\bar{z}}$. By so doing, K equals the cross product of the crude latent validities and the output covariance can now be expressed as a function of K:

$$cov_i(yz) = p_i q_i K. \tag{3.10}$$

If we could solve this equation for each x-slab we could also determine the grand taxon base rate by straightforward algebra. However, without further information, this equation cannot be solved because the number of known values (the output covariance) is less than the number of unknowns (p_i and K; remember $q_i = 1 - p_i$). Knowing even one p_i would allow us to solve the equation in the general case (over x-slabs) because K is a constant. Fortunately, we do have a good estimate of one p_i. Remember that in the x-slab containing the hitmax score, $p_i \approx .50$, and $p_i q_i \approx .25$. This implies that at the hitmax (h) interval,

$$cov_h(yz) = \frac{1}{4} K.$$

and by simple rearrangement

$$K = 4cov_h(yz). \tag{3.11}$$

Having determined K, we can now solve for the remaining p_i. Remembering that $q_i = 1 - p_i$:

$$cov_i(yz) = (p_i - p_i^2)K, \tag{3.12}$$

then

$$Kp_i^2 - Kp_i + cov_i(yz) = 0. \tag{3.13}$$

Equation (3.13) is a quadratic in p_i and can be solved by a well-known method.[4] The quadratic has two roots: We choose the smaller root for x-slabs below the hitmax cut and the larger root for x-slabs above the hitmax cut. Then, for each subsample, we multiply the conditional taxon rate by the x-slab sample size to estimate n_{ti}, the number of taxon members in each x-slab. Next, we total the resulting values to estimate N_t, the number of taxon members in the total sample. Finally, we divide N_t by the total sample size, N, to calculate the grand taxon base rate:

$$P = (\Sigma n_{ti})/N.$$

[In these equations, replace $1 - p_i$ for p_i, and n_{ci} for n_{ti}, to calculate the x-slab- and total-sample-proportions for nontaxon members.]

In our running example, we have let x function as an input variable and y and z as output variables. To complete this study, we must repeat the aforementioned steps of this chapter two additional times: letting y func-

---

[4]
$$x = \frac{-b \pm \sqrt{b^2 - 4ac}}{2a}.$$

In terms of our example, $a = K$, $b = -K$, and $c = cov_i(yz)$. Thus, the two roots of the quadratic are obtained by solving

$$p_i = \frac{K \pm \sqrt{K^2 - 4Kcov_i(yz)}}{2K}.$$

tion as an input variable in the first analysis and z as an input variable in the second analysis. These additional analyses are conducted, in part, to estimate the hitmax and other parameters for *y* and *z*. After completing these runs we would have three nonredundant estimates of the taxon base rate. In later analyses, we can use the average (or median) of these estimates as our best value for *P*. The variance of the estimates is also an informative quantity that can be used as a MAXCOV *consistency test*.

MAXCOV Consistency Tests and Model Corroboration

We have stated that MAXCOV can be performed whenever three or more indicators are available and at least one indicator is measured on a continuous scale. Because MAXCOV works with covariances, the order of the output variables is immaterial ($cov(yz) = cov(zy)$). Hence, with three indicators—*x*, *y*, and *z*—three nonredundant MAXCOV analyses are possible:

MAXCOV 1		MAXCOV 2		MAXCOV 3	
input	*output*	*input*	*output*	*input*	*output*
x	y z	y	z x	z	x y

With *v* variables, $v \geq 3$, we can perform

$$M = v \times \frac{(v-1)!}{(v-3)! \; 2!}$$

MAXCOV analyses and generate *M* estimates of the taxon base rate. If the taxonic conjecture is correct, the *M* estimates should fall within a limited range of the [0, 1] probability continuum because each value is an estimate of the same parameter, *P*.

The variance of the *M* estimated base rates is a natural index for assessing the verisimilitude of a taxonic model. When the variance is small, the taxonic conjecture is supported. When the variance is sizable— as it will be whenever the base rate estimates randomly fall along the [0, 1] probability continuum—the taxonic conjecture is discorroborated.

These remarks are worth emphasizing because they illustrate our approach to MAXCOV model confirmation in particular and taxometric theory testing in general. When testing taxonic conjectures we prefer *consistency tests* over statistical tests because replication—provided by converging parameter estimates—grants stronger evidentiary support than small test statistics (assuming taxonicity is our null hypothesis) and associated large p values. In Chapter 7, we discuss the role of consistency tests in taxometric research at greater length. Here, we simply describe several consistency tests for MAXCOV. We have already described one such test: the variance of the estimated base rates. We now describe a second test.

With three taxon indicators, as in our example, we can compute six (nonredundant) *observed* and six *predicted* covariances (three covariances are also variances, that is, the covariance of a variable with itself).[5] Let S and $\hat{S}$ denote the observed and predicted covariance matrices for our example indicators. Then,

$$S = \begin{bmatrix} var(x) & cov(xy) & cov(xz) \\ cov(yx) & var(y) & cov(yz) \\ cov(zx) & cov(zy) & var(z) \end{bmatrix}$$

and

$$\hat{S} = \begin{bmatrix} Pvar(x_t) + Qvar(x_c) + PQ\Delta_{\bar{x}}^2 & PQ\Delta_{\bar{x}}\Delta_{\bar{y}} & PQ\Delta_{\bar{x}}\Delta_{\bar{z}} \\ PQ\Delta_{\bar{y}}\Delta_{\bar{x}} & Pvar(y_t) + Qvar(y_c) + PQ\Delta_{\bar{y}}^2 & PQ\Delta_{\bar{y}}\Delta_{\bar{z}} \\ PQ\Delta_{\bar{z}}\Delta_{\bar{x}} & PQ\Delta_{\bar{z}}\Delta_{\bar{y}} & Pvar(z_t) + Qvar(z_c) + PQ\Delta_{\bar{z}}^2 \end{bmatrix}.$$

If (a) the taxonic hypothesis is correct *and* (b) the MAXCOV auxiliary conjectures are satisfied *and* (c) the taxonic parameters are estimated without error (i.e., sampling error), then the difference matrix, $S_D = S - \hat{S}$, will be a null matrix. Obviously, we do not expect this idealized result with real data because the aforementioned conjuncture will rarely hold. Rather, we consider our taxonic and associated auxiliary conjectures corroborated whenever S and $\hat{S}$ are reasonably close. But how are we to define "reasonably close" in this context? We do not have an exact numerical definition

---

[5] In the absence of nuisance covariance, Equation (3.9) implies that the amount of each variable's variance that arises from the taxonic mixture is given by

$$\frac{cov(xy) \cdot cov(xz)}{cov(yz)} = PQ\Delta_x^2.$$

This quantity is analogous to the communality in the (dimensional) linear factor analysis model. With more than three variables, multiple "taxonic" communalities can be estimated and averaged for each variable.

for this phrase, although we are able to derive some rules of thumb for evaluating the *consistency* of S and $\hat{S}$.

Recently, we have experimented with a goodness-of-fit index, called the GFI (Jöreskog & Sörbom, 1988), as one index from a battery of consistency tests to evaluate taxonic fit. The GFI was originally introduced in the structural equation modeling literature (see Tanaka & Huba, 1989, for a review) and it is used frequently in that context. The index is given by

$$GFI = 1 - \frac{tr[S(\hat{S}^{-1}) - I]^2}{tr[S(\hat{S}^{-1})]^2}, \qquad (3.14)$$

where I equals an identity matrix and tr denotes the trace operator (the sum of diagonal elements; Graybill, 1983). The GFI has a simple interpretation. It can be viewed as a multivariate R^2 or coefficient of determination (Tanaka & Huba, 1989). Values of this index range from 0.00 to 1.00, with higher values indicating better fit. In a small Monte Carlo study of the GFI, we recently found that taxonic samples generally produce GFI values greater than .90 whereas dimensional samples rarely produce values in this range when S and $\hat{S}$ are defined as above.

Allocating Individuals to Taxonic Classes

We have learned how to estimate key taxonic parameters and have seen how to evaluate our estimates with consistency tests. Suppose, for indicators x, y, and z, our parameter estimates have passed a series of consistency hurdles and we wish to identify the taxon members in our sample. There are several methods for doing so. A statistically powerful method uses Bayes's Theorem[6] (Meehl, 1973a, p. 214) to derive taxon membership probabilities for the 2^v possible response patterns that can be formed when v indicators are dichotomized at their hitmax cuts. To use Bayes's Theorem in this context we need an estimate of P, the grand taxon base rate, and estimates of the valid (p_{tx}) and false (p_{cx}) positive rates for each taxon indicator. We have already seen how to estimate P. We now define the valid

---

[6]Bayes's Theorem was published posthumously in a Memoir to the Royal Society of London (Bayes, 1763) by the 18th-century English clergyman Thomas Bayes. One common form of the theorem is

$$Pr(A|B) = \frac{Pr(A)(Pr(B|A)}{Pr(B)}.$$

and false positive rates and illustrate how to estimate these useful parameters.

The *valid positive rate* (p_{tx}) for indicator x is the probability that a *taxon* member scores higher than the hitmax on x. In some literatures this parameter is called the indicator sensitivity rate. The *false positive rate* (p_{cx}) for x is the probability that a *nontaxon* member scores higher than the hitmax on x. Thus, the false positive rate is the obverse of the indicator specificity rate. These discrimination indexes are easily calculated from previously defined MAXCOV output.

Let n_{t_h} denote the number of taxon members in the hitmax-interval x-slab, and $n_{t_{i>h}}$ the number of taxon members in a higher x-slab. Then, for any indicator, x, we can calculate the indicator valid and false positive rates as follows:

$$p_{tx} = \frac{.5(n_{t_h}) + \Sigma n_{t_{i>h}}}{N_t}, \quad \textit{valid positive rate} \tag{3.14}$$

$$p_{cx} = \frac{.5(n_{c_h}) + \Sigma n_{c_{i>h}}}{N_c}, \quad \textit{false positive rate} \tag{3.15}$$

To illustrate these ideas, suppose a hypothetical subject, named Butch, scores higher than the hitmax on indicators x and z and lower than the hitmax on indicator y. Bayes's Theorem implies that the inverse probability (Pr) that Butch belongs to the taxon class is given by

$$Pr(t|x^+y^-z^+) = \frac{Pp_{tx}q_{ty}p_{tz}}{Pp_{tx}q_{ty}p_{tz} + Qp_{cx}q_{cy}p_{cz}}.$$

Another subject, Mabel, scores lower than the hitmax on x and y and higher than the hitmax on z. This implies that Mabel's taxon membership probability is given by

$$Pr(t|x^-y^-z^+) = \frac{Pq_{tx}q_{ty}p_{tz}}{Pq_{tx}q_{ty}p_{tz} + Qq_{cx}q_{cy}p_{cz}}.$$

With three variables, eight score patterns are possible: $(+ + +)$, $(+ + -)$, $(+ - +)$, . . . , $(- - -)$.[7] For each pattern there is a Bayes's posterior probability of belonging to the taxon class. We can derive a general equation for these estimates by defining a selection variable, θ, where $\theta = 1$ if an individual scores higher than the hitmax cut on indicator i, and 0 otherwise. Let RP denote an individual's item response pattern on v taxon indicators. Furthermore, let pt_i denote the valid positive rate and pc_i the false positive rate for indicator i, $i = 1, 2, 3, . . . v$. Then, according to Bayes's Theorem, the posterior probability of belonging to the taxon class for response pattern RP equals

$$Pr(t|RP) = \frac{P\prod_{i=1}^{v} pt_i^{\theta} qt_i^{1-\theta}}{P\prod_{t=1}^{v} pt_i^{\theta} qt_i^{1-\theta} + Q\prod_{i=1}^{v} pc_i^{\theta} qc_i^{1-\theta}} \tag{3.16}$$

where $\prod$ is the cumulative product operator.

We assign individuals to the taxon class if their taxon membership score, $PR(t|RP)$, exceeds a predefined threshold value. For example, to minimize false positive and false negative assignments in our sample, we assign individuals with membership scores of .50 and higher to the taxon class and all others to the complement class. Suppose, however, that we wish to minimize false positive assignments (i.e., incorrectly assigning a nontaxon member to the taxon class) and we are willing to tolerate an increase in false negative assignments. In this case we would simply raise our cut score for calling someone a taxon member.

When classifying individuals into latent taxa we work with membership scores that have been dichotomized. Also important is that the *non*dichotomized scores are informative as they provide a means of corroborating our taxonic model. If the data measure a latent taxon, the distribution of taxon membership scores will look like a U, with a marked dip in the middle of the distribution and a buildup of scores at the distribution extremes. This distinctive shape is not found with dimensional indicators because the

---

[7]We have written an *S*-Plus routine called COMB that calculates all possible combinations for v variables. The source code for COMB is found in Appendix B.

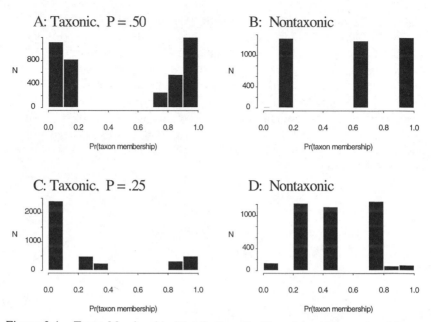

Figure 3.4.   Taxon Membership Distributions for Taxonic and Dimensional Data

estimated probabilities do not correspond to latent parameters. In other words, if there is no taxon, the estimated taxon membership probabilities do not denote and their distribution is typically uniform across the [0, 1] probability continuum. To illustrate these points, we calculated taxon membership scores for the four data sets used for Figure 3.3 and plotted these scores in the histograms shown in Figure 3.4. Notice, in this figure, that for the taxonic samples the majority of membership probabilities fall within the outer deciles of the probability continuum and for the dimensional samples the probabilities are more evenly distributed.

4

MAXEIG-HITMAX: A Multivariate Generalization of MAXCOV

Taxonomists have always had the reputation of being difficult.

—W. W. Moss (1983, p. 73)

Coherent cut kinetics (Meehl & Yonce, 1994, 1996) is the name we use to describe an important set of procedures for determining whether a data set is taxonic or not. Each word in this rubric describes a fundamental property of these taxometric techniques. For instance, the word "coherent" implies that something is logically ordered. To "cut" something is to separate it into parts. And "kinetics" implies movement or pertaining to motion. In coherent cut kinetics, "we *move cuts* on a designated input variable and study the statistical behavior of other (output) variables on cases in the region of the *cut* and in regions demarcated by the cut" (Meehl & Yonce, 1996, p. 1092, emphasis added). Taxonicity is inferred when the output-variable summary statistics are *logically ordered.*

In Chapter 3, we described a technique, called MAXCOV-HITMAX, that is representative of the coherent cut kinetics method. The focus of this chapter is on MAXEIG-HITMAX, a related technique that also belongs to this family of procedures. Our goal in this chapter is to demonstrate that MAXEIG is the logical multivariate generalization of MAXCOV. In MAXEIG we move from the bivariate to the multivariate realm by using conditional eigenvalues in the same way that we used conditional covariances in MAXCOV. To demonstrate the utility of this new approach, in the following sections we analyze a small data set with MAXEIG. To keep the example simple, we use biological sex as our taxonic variable.

31

Separating the Boys From the Girls

Separating the boys from the girls is a form of *blatant class* analysis because there are well-known methods for assigning individuals to taxonic groups that do not involve taxometric procedures—*unless, of course, you are from another planet.* Imagine, if you will, that a psychometrician from planet Ταχθη has been sent to Earth to determine whether earthlings come in two types. As luck would have it, even with her three eyes and two brains, she finds that all earthlings look alike. Fortunately, our galactic psychometrician is from an advanced civilization with highly developed taxometric procedures. So shortly after touchdown she locates the nearest shopping mall and hands a clipboard-secured questionnaire to 40 adolescents. In this questionnaire she inquires about three variables: hair length, hip-to-waist ratio, and knowledge of flowers (these variables were mentioned in an old epic poem that described earthling mating rituals). The data for this hypothetical study are reported in Table 4.1. Unbeknown to our interstellar traveler, they were gathered from 20 boys (B) and 20 girls (G).

We also analyze these data to determine whether a taxonic model adequately accounts for the covariance relations among the conjectured taxon indicators.[1] As a first step, let us look at the univariate histograms and smoothed density plots that are shown in Figure 4.1. Notice that the score distributions for two of our variables, hair length and knowledge of flowers, show no signs of bimodality or other obvious characteristics of two-group mixture distributions. The distribution for the remaining variable, hip-to-waist ratio, is suggestive of bimodality, but even here it is difficult to draw firm conclusions because we are working with only 40

---

[1]The data were generated so that the indicator means for the boys were uniformly .50 and for the girls uniformly .70. The within-taxa standard deviations for all variables were constrained to equal .10. Thus, on each variable the groups were separated by 2 within-class standard deviations. Moreover, the within-group correlation matrices were constrained to equal identity matrices (i.e., ones on the diagonal and zeros elsewhere). Note that we did not sample from populations with these characteristics. We constrained the 40 observation vectors to satisfy these conditions by generating the data using these six steps for each group: (1) Generate X, an $N \times P$ matrix of random normal deviates, where N equals the desired sample size and P equals the desired number of observed variables; (2) calculate C, the population covariance matrix of X; (3) compute T, where T is the Choleski square root factor of C, $(C = TT')$; (4) construct Σ, the desired covariance matrix; (5) compute A, where A is the Choleski square root factor of Σ, $(\Sigma = AA')$; and (6) the model-implied matrix of raw responses, Y is given by $Y = X (T^{-1})' A'$. The data reported in Table 4.1 differ slightly from their model-implied values because of round-off and truncation error when converting them to t-scores.

TABLE 4.1 Example Data and Latent Group Summary Statistics for 20 Boys (B) and 20 Girls (G)

Boys

ID	Hair Length	Xc1	Hip-to-Waist	Xc2	Know Flowers	Xc3
B 1	59	-2.77	79	17.85	50	-9.65
B 2	61	-0.77	49	-12.15	60	0.35
B 3	43	-18.77	43	-18.15	44	-15.65
B 4	59	-2.77	58	-3.15	62	2.35
B 5	60	-1.77	50	-11.15	52	-7.65
B 6	52	-9.77	53	-8.15	42	-17.65
B 7	25	-36.78	54	-7.15	56	-3.65
B 8	64	2.23	41	-20.15	60	0.35
B 9	60	-1.77	59	-2.15	45	-14.65
B 10	55	-6.77	64	2.85	55	-4.65
B 11	36	-25.78	52	-9.15	58	-1.65
B 12	55	-6.77	39	-22.15	55	-4.65
B 13	65	3.23	51	-10.15	45	-14.65
B 14	55	-6.77	55	-6.15	57	-2.65
B 15	62	0.23	32	-29.15	56	-3.65
B 16	48	-13.77	47	-14.15	43	-16.65
B 17	62	0.23	48	-13.15	34	-25.65
B 18	53	-8.77	48	-13.15	28	-31.65
B 19	46	-15.77	46	-15.15	36	-23.65
B 20	52	-9.77	41	-20.15	63	3.35
M	53.60		50.45		50.05	
SD	10.04		10.06		9.97	

R			
	1.00		
	.00	1.00	
	.00	-.01	1.00

Girls

ID	Hair Length	Xc1	Hip-to-Waist	Xc2	Know Flowers	Xc3
G 21	83	21.22	68	6.85	63	3.35
G 22	66	4.23	78	16.85	59	-0.65
G 23	71	9.23	74	12.85	56	-3.65
G 24	91	29.22	61	-0.15	70	10.35
G 25	68	6.23	67	5.85	65	5.35
G 26	55	-6.77	62	0.85	57	-2.65
G 27	63	1.23	72	10.85	86	26.35
G 28	62	0.23	90	28.85	56	-3.65
G 29	64	2.23	76	14.85	71	11.35
G 30	88	26.22	81	19.85	78	18.35
G 31	64	2.23	70	8.85	78	18.35
G 32	65	3.23	65	3.85	67	7.35
G 33	83	21.22	79	17.85	70	10.35
G 34	67	5.23	87	25.85	68	8.35
G 35	80	18.23	65	3.85	63	3.35
G 36	60	-1.77	50	-11.15	72	12.35
G 37	65	3.23	63	1.85	68	8.35
G 38	61	-0.77	81	19.85	94	34.35
G 39	70	8.23	83	21.85	65	5.35
G 40	73	11.23	65	3.85	79	19.35
M	69.95		71.85		69.25	
SD	9.96		10.04		9.95	

R			
	1.00		
	.02	1.00	
	-.01	.00	1.00

NOTE: M = mean; SD = standard deviation; R = correlations; and Xc_i = deviation scores for indicator i.

33

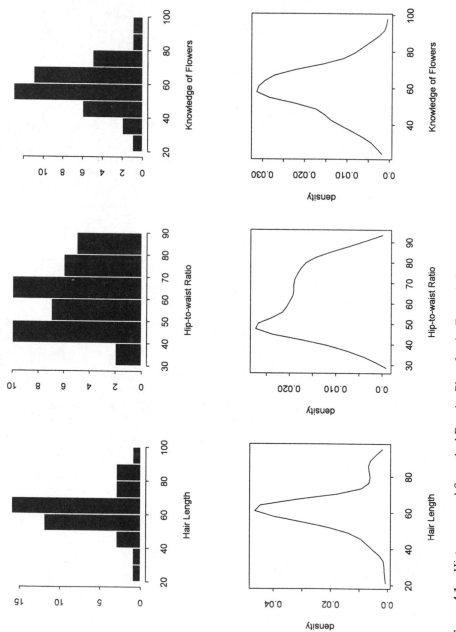

Figure 4.1. Histograms and Smoothed Density Plots for the Example Data

observations. Perhaps the joint distribution will reveal more subtle patterns in the data.

The 3-dimensional structure of these data can be graphically depicted in several ways. One way is simply to plot the raw scores in a 3-dimensional point cloud. Another is to first transform the scores into a potentially more informative configuration before plotting them. For instance, using a principal components analysis, we can transform the correlated scores into uncorrelated scores. By doing so we lose none of the information in the data, and in some cases the new configuration reveals patterns that were not easily seen in the original scores.

Principal component scores can be calculated from (a) raw scores, (b) deviation scores, or (c) standardized deviation scores (see Green, 1978, chap. 8). The weight matrix that transforms these scores into uncorrelated principal component scores is obtained from an eigendecomposition of a sum-of-squares-and-cross-products matrix (SSCP). In the present example, we work with deviation scores, and thus the appropriate cross products matrix is a covariance matrix.

Let $\mathbf{X}$ represent the matrix of raw scores that are shown in Table 4.1, and let $\mathbf{X}_c$ denote the deviation scores (centered scores) that are also shown in the table. Then, the covariance matrix of $\mathbf{X}$ (or $\mathbf{X}_c$) is given by

$$C = \mathbf{X}_c' \mathbf{X}_c \frac{1}{N-1}.$$

For the example data we find that

$$
C = \begin{array}{ccc}
\text{Hair Length} & \text{Hip/Waist} & \text{Flowers} \\
\left[\begin{array}{ccc}
165.922 & 90.445 & 80.329 \\
 & 215.823 & 105.054 \\
 & & 191.156
\end{array}\right]
\end{array}.
$$

Using well-known theory (e.g., Jackson, 1991), this covariance matrix—like any SSCP matrix—can be decomposed into a triple product of eigenvalues ($\mathbf{L}$) and eigenvectors ($\mathbf{U}$). Before defining these terms, we illustrate them using our example data. For the above covariance matrix it can be shown that

$$\mathbf{C} = \begin{matrix} & \mathbf{U} \\ & \begin{bmatrix} .495 & -.090 & .864 \\ .649 & -.622 & -.437 \\ .577 & .777 & -.249 \end{bmatrix} \end{matrix} \times \begin{matrix} & \mathbf{L} \\ & \begin{bmatrix} 378.199 & 0 & 0 \\ 0 & 97.72 & 0 \\ 0 & 0 & 96.98 \end{bmatrix} \end{matrix} \times \begin{matrix} & \mathbf{U'} \\ & \begin{bmatrix} .495 & .649 & .577 \\ -.090 & -.622 & .777 \\ .864 & -.437 & -.249 \end{bmatrix} \end{matrix}.$$

The eigenvectors, contained in $\mathbf{U}$, represent one set of weights for rotating the original scores into uncorrelated principal component scores ($\mathbf{Z}$). Notice that the original scores are moderately correlated in the total sample:

$$\mathbf{R} = \begin{matrix} \text{Hair Length} & \text{Hip/Waist} & \text{Flowers} \\ \begin{bmatrix} 1.000 & .478 & .451 \\ & 1.000 & .517 \\ & & 1.000 \end{bmatrix} \end{matrix}.$$

When we postmultiply $\mathbf{X}_c$ by $\mathbf{U}$, however, such that

$$\mathbf{Z} = \mathbf{X}_c \mathbf{U},$$

the transformed scores are uncorrelated. Suppose that instead of correlating the component scores we compute covariances. Doing so yields

$$\mathbf{C}_z = \frac{1}{N-1} \mathbf{Z'Z} = \mathbf{L} = \begin{bmatrix} 378.199 & 0 & 0 \\ 0 & 97.72 & 0 \\ 0 & 0 & 96.98 \end{bmatrix}.$$

The above expression helps us understand the meaning of an eigenvalue because it demonstrates that the variances of the principal component scores are equivalent to the eigenvalues of the raw-score covariance matrix. Notice in this equation that the eigenvalues are ordered such that the variance explained by the first component is larger than (or equal) to that explained by the second, which in turn is larger than that of the third, and so on. This is an important and common feature of component scores.

In some situations, it is convenient to work with standardized component scores ($\mathbf{Z}_s$) with unit standard deviations and means of 0.00. In these situations, standardization is easily accomplished once it is recognized that the square roots of the eigenvalues equal the standard deviations of the component scores. Hence,

TABLE 4.2 Principal Component Scores (Z) and Standardized Principal Component Scores (Z_s) for the Example Data

	Boys							Girls					
ID	Z_1	Z_{s1}	Z_2	Z_{s2}	Z_3	Z_{s3}	ID	Z_1	Z_{s1}	Z_2	Z_{s2}	Z_3	Z_{s3}
B 1	4.646	0.239	-18.362	-1.857	-7.792	-0.791	G 21	16.890	0.869	-3.576	-0.362	14.511	1.474
B 2	-8.071	-0.415	7.904	0.800	4.554	0.462	G 22	12.657	0.651	-11.374	-1.151	-3.552	-0.361
B 3	-30.115	-1.549	0.825	0.083	-4.386	-0.445	G 23	10.804	0.556	-11.669	-1.180	3.266	0.332
B 4	-2.063	-0.106	4.038	0.408	-1.607	-0.163	G 24	20.347	1.046	5.500	0.556	22.737	2.309
B 5	-12.535	-0.645	1.152	0.117	5.248	0.533	G 25	9.969	0.513	-0.044	-0.004	1.487	0.151
B 6	-20.321	-1.045	-7.767	-0.786	-0.481	-0.049	G 26	-4.332	-0.223	-1.977	-0.200	-5.565	-0.565
B 7	-24.957	-1.283	4.934	0.499	-27.742	-2.817	G 27	22.863	1.176	13.623	1.378	-10.258	-1.042
B 8	-11.780	-0.606	12.613	1.276	10.643	1.081	G 28	16.736	0.861	-20.814	-2.106	-11.505	-1.168
B 9	-10.732	-0.552	-9.891	-1.001	3.061	0.311	G 29	17.296	0.889	-0.619	-0.063	-7.400	-0.751
B 10	-4.188	-0.215	-4.777	-0.483	-5.940	-0.603	G 30	36.466	1.875	-0.457	-0.046	9.407	0.955
B 11	-19.655	-1.011	6.740	0.682	-17.862	-1.814	G 31	17.442	0.897	8.557	0.866	-6.524	-0.662
B 12	-20.421	-1.050	10.783	1.091	4.987	0.506	G 32	8.340	0.429	3.027	0.306	-0.730	-0.074
B 13	-13.451	-0.692	-5.364	-0.543	10.878	1.105	G 33	28.074	1.444	-4.980	-0.504	7.957	0.808
B 14	-8.877	-0.456	2.379	0.241	-2.505	-0.254	G 34	24.192	1.244	-10.069	-1.019	-8.867	-0.900
B 15	-20.923	-1.076	15.285	1.546	13.846	1.406	G 35	13.457	0.692	-1.438	-0.145	13.230	1.343
B 16	-25.620	-1.317	-2.894	-0.293	-1.564	-0.159	G 36	-0.989	-0.051	16.702	1.690	0.258	0.026
B 17	-23.235	-1.195	-11.778	-1.191	12.342	1.253	G 37	7.618	0.392	5.049	0.511	-0.105	-0.011
B 18	-31.155	-1.602	-15.630	-1.581	6.062	0.616	G 38	32.335	1.663	14.421	1.459	-17.916	-1.819
B 19	-31.301	-1.610	-7.533	-0.762	-1.109	-0.113	G 39	21.348	1.098	-10.183	-1.030	-3.778	-0.384
B 20	-15.989	-0.822	16.029	1.621	-0.475	-0.048	G 40	19.228	0.989	11.634	1.177	3.189	0.324

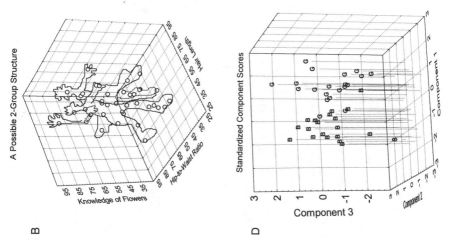

A   Raw Data

B   A Possible 2-Group Structure

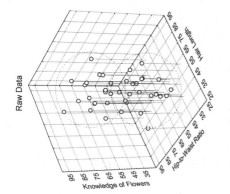

C   Unstandardized Component Scores

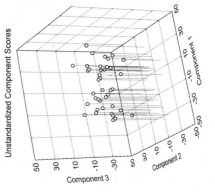

D   Standardized Component Scores

Figure 4.2.   Four Possible Ways of Plotting the Example Data

$$\mathbf{Z}_s = \mathbf{X}_c \mathbf{U} \mathbf{L}^{-\frac{1}{2}}.$$

Perhaps at this point you are asking yourself, *what does all of this have to do with taxometrics?* A straightforward answer to that question is provided in Table 4.2 and Figure 4.2.

Table 4.2 reports the principal component scores ($\mathbf{Z}$) and the standardized component scores ($\mathbf{Z}_s$) for the 40 cases of our hypothetical study. As you scan this table, pay particular attention to the columns labeled $\mathbf{Z}_1$ and $\mathbf{Z}_{s1}$. These columns contain the scores on the first principal component. It is easy to discern a pattern in these scores. For boys, the majority of scores are below 0.00, whereas for girls, the majority are above 0.00. In other words, in either metric, the component scores are clearly patterned in a manner that is consistent with the gender status of the examinees. Another way of seeing this pattern is to look at the 3-dimensional scatterplots of the raw and transformed data.

Figure 4.2 shows four possible ways of plotting these data. The first panel demonstrates how the point cloud of the raw scores approximates an ellipsoid in the cube defined by the three axes. This elongated football is the graphical representation of the positive manifold in the indicator correlation matrix. Notice that if we stare long enough at these points we can also discern the outlines of two overlapping clusters (emphasized by the dashed circles in the plot). If this clumping was more obvious, we might conclude that we were working with a mixture of two samples rather than with a single sample. Of course, if we stare even longer, we can "see" many interesting patterns in this point cloud, or for that matter, in cumulus clouds, starry skies, or Rorschach inkblots. For instance, Panel B illustrates a particularly dynamic relationship between the points which, interestingly enough, also supports our taxonic hypothesis. However, as clinically trained psychologists we realize that such structures may represent nothing more than fanciful projections of creative minds, and thus we require more cogent evidence of taxonicity.

Panel C in Figure 4.2, which shows the unstandardized principal component scores, provides such evidence. Notice in this plot that the taxonic structure of the data is clearly revealed by the clustered dispersion of the points on the first principal component. The other components provide little help in recognizing this structure. As a general rule, when a pool of indicators covary for reasons described by the reduced form of the General Covariance Mixture Theorem (see Equation [3.9]), the first principal component of the indicator covariance matrix will reveal the taxonicity of the data. Accordingly, the first eigenvalue of the covariance matrix will be large, relative to the other eigenvalues, because taxonicity increases the variance of the component scores on the first dimension. Remember that the eigenvalues also represent the variances of the unstandardized component scores.

The last panel in Figure 4.2 shows the scatterplot of the standardized component scores. It also shows that by equating the variances of the scores we have increased the scatter on the second and third components relative to the first. Importantly, we have not distorted the two-group structure that was first seen in the previous plot. In Chapter 5, we describe some important reasons why standardizing component scores (and factor scores) is useful when working with taxonic data. In the present case, however, we standardized the scores for a relatively mundane reason: It was easier to read the labels in the plot. These labels are important because they signify the gender of the 40 examinees: B denotes a male, G a female.

Suppose we call any person with $Z_{s1} > 0$ a female and all other persons a male. Scanning the labels in Panel D allows us to quickly assess the accuracy of this classification rule. After tallying the labels we find that this simple rule correctly classifies 37 out of 40 individuals, a number which corresponds to a hit rate of 0.925. We can also use this method to estimate the taxon base rate, and our estimated base rate equals .475. This value is comfortably close to the true base rate, .50.

In Chapter 3, we saw that the conditional covariance between taxon indicators is greatest in the range of the conditioning variable (which we called the input variable) that includes an even number of taxon and complement members (i.e., where $p_i = .50$). From comments in the previous paragraphs it should now be obvious that conditional eigenvalues of a covariance matrix will also be largest in this range. Consequently, conditional eigenvalues can be used with multivariate data in the same way that conditional covariances are used in MAXCOV-HITMAX. A plot of conditional eigenvalues is called a MAXEIG-HITMAX plot. We have found these plots to be extremely helpful when distinguishing taxonic from non-taxonic data, and in the next section we describe how to make a MAXEIG plot, using the example data from our galactic psychometrician.

Using MAXEIG to Separate the Boys From the Girls

A few sentences back we claimed that conditional eigenvalues from a covariance matrix can be used to construct a MAXEIG-HITMAX plot. In truth, that claim was not correct. The problem here is that the eigenvalues are complicated functions of *all* of the covariances, including the covariances of the variables with themselves. In other words, the conditional *variances* of the indicators also influence the relative size of the eigenvalues. This unwanted source of variation is particularly problematic in situations where the variances differ markedly in the taxon and complement groups. For instance, in a recent taxometric study of dissociative experiences (e.g., Waller, Putnam, & Carlson, 1996), which we discuss more fully in Chapter 6, the indicator variances in the taxon group were several times larger than the variances in the nontaxon group.

A simple, although highly effective, way of removing the influence of the variances on the conditional eigenvalues is to remove the variances from the conditional covariance matrices, by setting the variances to zero. After doing so, the matrix is no longer Gramian[2]—because a variable cannot covary with other variables if it does not covary with itself—but it still has computable eigenvalues. Moreover, these eigenvalues are obviously a function of only the covariances. To illustrate how this idea works, we will now demonstrate a MAXEIG analysis on the example data.

As you may recall, the true base rate in this example is .50 because the sample is made up of 20 boys and 20 girls. Notice that we only have 40 observations in the total sample. MAXEIG handles small samples by using *overlapping windows* on the input variable. The amount of overlap between windows determines the number of cases in each window. Thus, by controlling the degree of overlap we can increase the stability of our estimated summary statistic (which in this case is an eigenvalue). We demonstrate this idea by using hair length as an input variable and by constructing 21 overlapping windows with 90% overlap.[3]

Constructing Overlapping Windows

Define **overlap** as the percentage overlap between contiguous windows; let **m.per.int** equal the approximate number of cases in each window; let **number** denote the desired number of windows that, when taken together, span the range of the input scores; and define **m.over** as the approximate number of overlapping cases between contiguous windows. Then, if **overlap** (% overlap) and **number** (# of windows) are specified in advance, we can determine **m.per.int** (# of cases in a window) and **m.over** (# of overlapping cases) by the expression

---

[2]A Gramian matrix is one that can be expressed as the product moment of another matrix. Thus, any SSCP matrix (e.g., a covariance or correlation matrix) will be Gramian.

[3]The formula we use is a slightly modified version of the *S*-Plus (StatSci, 1996) **equal.counts** function.

m.per.int = (N) / (number × (1 - overlap) + overlap)

and

m.over = overlap × m.per.int,

where N equals the total sample size. For the sorted input scores, the appropriate ordinal positions for the lower and upper boundary points of the overlapping windows are given by the following:

    For i in 0 to (**number** − 1)
        lower = i × (**m.per.int** − **m.over**) +1,
        upper = (i + **number** − 1) × (**m.per.int** − **m.over**) + **m.over**.

In the present example, this formula yields the 21 pairs of endpoints that are shown in Table 4.3.

Table 4.3 also reports the maximum eigenvalues from the 21 modified covariance matrices that were formed from the cases falling within the 21 overlapping windows. Consistent with a base rate of .50, the maximum eigenvalues of these matrices are smallish at the extremes of the sorted input scores and rise to a peak toward the midpoint of the score distribution. Finally, the last column in the table shows the eigenvalues after smoothing them with a running medians smoother (Tukey, 1977).

A MAXEIG plot is a plot of the smoothed eigenvalues versus the midpoints of the (possibly) overlapping windows. The peak of this plot identifies the hitmax point for the same reason that the peak of a MAXCOV plot identifies the hitmax on the sorted input scores. Under the assumption that the component distributions of the commingled sample are symmetrical, we can also use the estimated hitmax to estimate the sample base rate. This is done by counting the number of cases that fall above the hitmax and then dividing this number by the total sample size. Because MAXCOV does not require this additional assumption, its parameter estimates may be more accurate in a wider range of circumstances. However, even in cases where the component distributions are not symmetrical, MAXEIG plots can still be used to garner strong support for a taxonic hypothesis because the differences between taxonic and nontaxonic MAXEIG plots are oftentimes quite stark.

Figure 4.3 contains the three MAXEIG plots for the example data. For all plots in this figure we constructed 21 overlapping windows with 90% overlap. Above each plot we also report the estimated base rate. Notice

TABLE 4.3 Twenty-One Overlapping Windows for Hair Length

Overlapping Windows	Endpoints		Number of Cases	Eigenvalues	
	Lower	Upper		Maximum λ	Smoothed Maximum l
1	−2.855	−0.215	14	0.177	0.173
2	−2.001	−0.138	16	0.200	0.186
3	−1.225	−0.138	14	0.193	0.204
4	−1.069	−0.138	13	0.116	0.247
5	−0.759	−0.060	14	0.366	0.303
6	−0.681	0.017	15	0.381	0.349
7	−0.526	0.017	14	0.294	0.380
8	−0.526	0.095	15	0.402	0.407
9	−0.526	0.173	18	0.444	0.441
10	−0.215	0.173	14	0.505	0.485
11	−0.215	0.250	17	0.473	0.543
12	−0.138	0.250	15	0.613	0.600
13	−0.138	0.250	15	0.613	0.623
14	−0.060	0.406	14	0.634	0.595
15	0.017	0.483	13	0.479	0.532
16	0.017	0.639	14	0.468	0.453
17	0.017	0.871	16	0.400	0.359
18	0.173	1.415	13	0.172	0.278
19	0.173	1.648	15	0.191	0.237
20	0.173	2.036	16	0.298	0.226
21	0.250	2.269	14	0.248	0.218

44

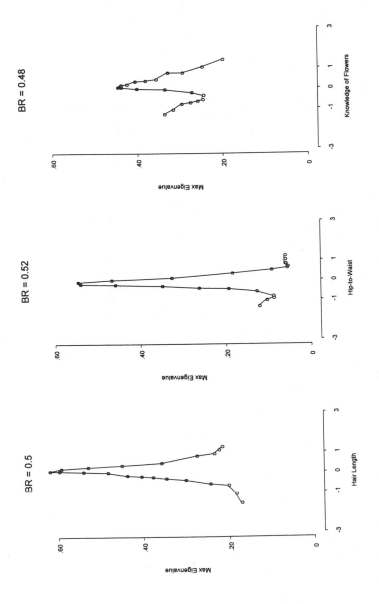

Figure 4.3. MAXEIG Plots for the Example Data

that even with 40 observations these estimates are very close to the known value, and the average of the estimates is precisely .50. Although MAXEIG performed remarkably well in this example, we remind the reader that the taxon and complement means were well separated and that all of the indicator covariation was due to the taxon-complement mix (i.e., nuisance covariance was absent). We do not recommend the use of MAXEIG, or any taxometric procedure, in smallish samples unless the above conditions are clearly satisfied.

As a final point, we describe a situation in which MAXEIG plots can be extremely informative even though the parameter estimates that are associated with those plots are slightly biased. The situation we are talking about concerns low base rate taxa. Specifically, we have found that when the taxon base rate is equal to or lower than .10, it can often be difficult to unambiguously detect taxonicity with MAXCOV-HITMAX plots because the MAXCOV function does not produce a clear cusp at the point of the hitmax. In these situations, a simple MAXEIG consistency test can often provide the needed information to judge whether a sample is truly taxonic. We call this test the "inchworm consistency test" for reasons that will be apparent shortly.

The Inchworm Consistency Test

The inchworm consistency test works as follows. We perform multiple MAXEIG analyses on a pool of output variables, each time using the same input variable. We begin with a small number of overlapping windows—say, 5 windows—with a moderate degree of overlap (we have found that 50% overlap often works well). We then perform another MAXEIG analysis, this time with a slightly greater number of overlapping windows. This process is repeated until we have approximately 80 windows. At that point, if the data are truly taxonic, then we should easily discern a pattern in the MAXEIG plots. Specifically, for taxonic data the plots will resemble a geometrid caterpillar ambulating across a deserted road. However, if the indicators tap a latent factor (dimension) rather than a latent class variable, the plots will resemble an inchworm that never made it across a busy highway. In other words, the inchworm will be flat! Figures 4.4 and 4.5 that complete this chapter illustrate this useful test.

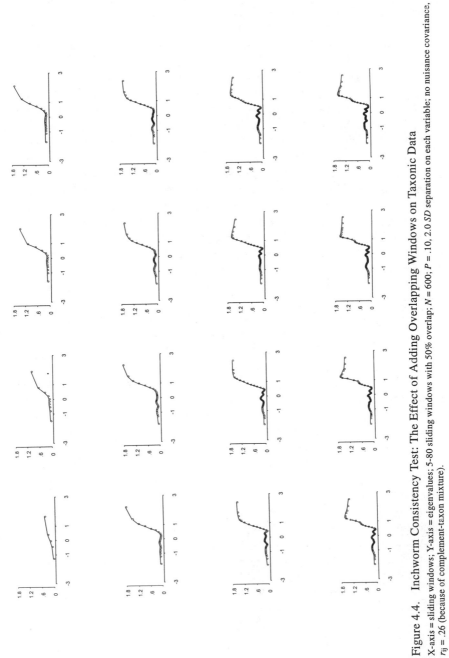

Figure 4.4. Inchworm Consistency Test: The Effect of Adding Overlapping Windows on Taxonic Data

X-axis = sliding windows; Y-axis = eigenvalues; 5-80 sliding windows with 50% overlap; $N = 600$; $P = .10$, 2.0 SD separation on each variable; no nuisance covariance, $r_{ij} = .26$ (because of complement-taxon mixture).

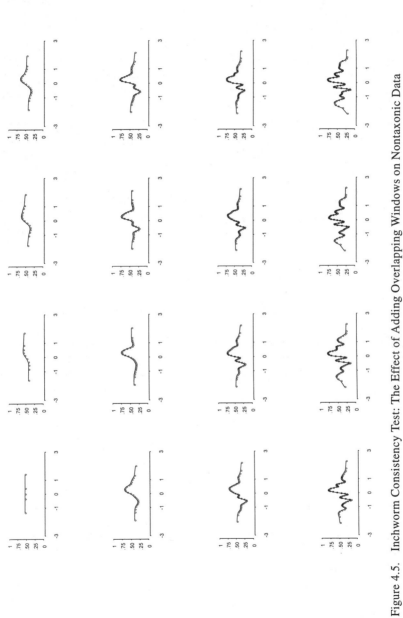

Figure 4.5. Inchworm Consistency Test: The Effect of Adding Overlapping Windows on Nontaxonic Data

X-axis = sliding windows; Y-axis = eigenvalues; 5-80 sliding windows with 50% overlap; $N = 600$; nontaxonic samples, $r_{ij} = .26$ (from factor loadings of .510 on all variables).

5 Factor-Analytic Techniques for Distinguishing Types From Continua: L-Mode

If the misapplication of factor methods continues at the present rate, we shall find general disappointment with the results because they are usually meaningless as far as psychological research interpretation is concerned.

—L. L. Thurstone (1937, p. 73)

Factor analysis is often described as a psychometric model for elucidating the latent *dimensional* structure of multivariate data. In this chapter and in Chapter 6, we show how the factor model can also clarify the latent *typological* structure of certain mixture distributions. To set the stage for this approach, we begin the chapter by exhuming some long forgotten ideas on typological factors by L. L. Thurstone. We then briefly discuss a related psychometric model for finding groups in data called latent profile analysis. These sections lay the mathematical foundations for a new taxometric procedure that we call L-Mode. As shown below, L-Mode calculates the taxonic parameters of two-group mixture distributions from the *latent modes* of a factor-score density plot. We demonstrate the utility of this method by comparing the relative performance of L-Mode and two widely used cluster algorithms (Ward's method and Average Linkage) in 350 data sets with known cluster structure. Throughout the chapter we rely on the General Covariance Mixture Theorem to reveal the conceptual and mathematical links among these seemingly different, but theoretically related, multivariate techniques.

Factor Analysis and Typological Factors

Conceptually, factor analysis is a multivariate regression model in which multiple observed variables are linearly or nonlinearly (McDonald, 1962; Waller, Tellegen, McDonald, & Lykken, 1996) regressed on one or more unobserved variables called factors.[1] The linear factor analysis model can be succinctly expressed in matrix notation by:

$$\mathbf{X}_{(N \times v)} = \xi_{(N \times k)} \, \Lambda'_{(k \times v)} + \eta_{(N \times v)} , \tag{5.1}$$

where

$\mathbf{X}$ is an N (subjects) by v (variables) matrix of observed scores
ξ is an N by k (factors) matrix of common factor scores
Λ is a v by k factor-pattern matrix with element $\lambda_{i,j}$ equal to the regression weight that results when variable i is regressed on factor j
η is an N by v matrix of unique factor scores.

As a simplification, we assume throughout the chapter that $\mathbf{X}$ contains deviation scores so that

$$\Sigma_{(x)} = \frac{\mathbf{X}'\mathbf{X}}{N-1} ,$$

where $\Sigma_{(x)}$ is the covariance matrix of $\mathbf{X}$. It is well known that, if the model holds, $\Sigma_{(x)}$ can also be expressed as a function of the factor parameters

$$\Sigma_{(x)} = \Lambda \Phi \Lambda' + \psi^2 , \tag{5.2}$$

where

Λ is defined as above
Φ is the covariance matrix for common factor scores
Ψ^2 is the diagonal matrix of variances for the unique factor scores (η); that is, $\Psi^2 = Diag(\Sigma_{(x)}) - Diag(\Lambda \Phi \Lambda')$.

When all latent factors are orthogonal (uncorrelated), Equation (5.2) can be further simplified:

---

[1]For a scholarly treatment of factor analysis, see Harman (1976); for a more gentle introduction, see Kim and Mueller (1978).

$$\Sigma_{(x)} = \Lambda\Lambda' + \psi^2 \tag{5.3}$$

Many researchers believe that factor scores are *necessarily* continuous. Factor score continuity, however, was not an original assumption of the model.[2] L. L. Thurstone, for example, believed that factors could also represent categorical variables, and in *The Vectors of Mind* (1935) he suggested that.

> It is conceivable, and not improbable, that some reference abilities will be found to be sufficiently elemental that they can be declared to be either present or absent in each individual without intermediate gradations in amount or degree of presence. . . . *If only two numerical values occur in the population for the standard scores in a primary ability, then the primary ability is a unitary ability.* This is a genetic interpretation of factors. (pp. 51-52)

Later, in the revised edition of *Vectors*—renamed *Multiple Factor Analysis* —Thurstone (1947) embellished on these ideas and added,

> A special case of the positive manifold is that in which each factor is either completely present or entirely absent in each member of the experimental population. Each individual member of the population has, then, one of only two possible standard scores—one positive, which represents the presence of the trait, and the other negative, which represents the complete absence of the trait. The numerical values of these two possible standard scores are determined by the proportion of the population that has the trait. (p. 343)

It is clear from these passages that Thurstone believed that factor scores could represent *dummy variables* in the sense described in Chapter 3 (e.g., Equation [3.5]). According to Thurstone, these dummy variables—or unitary factors, as he called them—have a direct genetic interpretation. To wit, they signify the presence or absence of a biological gene, and the complexity of mental traits is due to "the number of unitary factors that demonstrably contribute to the variance of the composite trait" (Thurstone, 1935, p. 206). Factors are not merely mathematical abstractions in this view; rather, they are quantitative analogues of hereditary influences (Thurstone, 1935, chap. 8, equations (17)–(25)).

---

[2]Note that factor-score continuity for common factors *is* an assumption of the maximum likelihood or generalized least squares parameter estimation techniques that are included in many statistical software packages (e.g., LISREL).

Of course, we now know that Thurstone's biometrical model of trait variation is badly flawed for several reasons, not the least of which is because the model fails to allow for environmental influences on trait covariation (see Waller & Shaver, 1994, for an example of the importance of the shared environment in behavioral variation). Nevertheless, Thurstone's intuition that factor analysis could be profitably used with discretely valued factor scores and that these factor scores could denote membership in latent taxa is an idea that merits reconsideration.[3] With the help of our imaginations let us consider one way in which Thurstone's idea can be developed further.

Suppose that in a mixed-gender sample we have collected data on the following variables: hair length, mean vocal pitch, chest girth, hip-to-waist ratio, psychometrically assessed sociability, fingernail length, and knowledge of flowers. Of course, these variables have little to nothing in common *except* one thing. They are all fallible indicators of biological gender because women typically score higher than men on these variables. Thus, for reasons formalized by the General Covariance Mixture Theorem, in a mixed-gender sample these indicators of the *gender taxon* will correlate positively. They will also define a *gender factor* in a factor analysis.

From the previously cited passages it is clear that Thurstone would have agreed with the above statements. He would have also known that the standardized factor scores on our gender factor can be expressed as simple functions of the relative number of females in our sample. That is, the factor scores are simple functions of the taxon base rate (P). Thurstone noted this idea in his first book on factor analysis (1935, chap. 8, equations (17)–(25)). His equations are somewhat complex but, fortunately, we can illustrate the logic of this method in a more straightforward manner.

Let an individual's nonstandardized factor score be denoted d_i. Define P as the unstandardized factor-score mean. Let $Q = 1 - P$; then $PQ = var(d)$. When standardized, the *true* factor scores, f_z, take on one of two values only (however, as discussed below, the estimated factor scores take on more than two values because of estimation error). For taxon members, d equals 1 and the standardized true factor score equals

$$f_{z_t} = \frac{d - P}{\sqrt{PQ}} = \frac{1 - P}{\sqrt{PQ}} = \frac{Q}{\sqrt{PQ}}.$$ (5.4)

---

[3]Gorsuch (1983, pp. 271-272) briefly mentions the possibility of "typological factor scores" but does not develop the idea further.

For nontaxon members, d equals 0 and

$$f_{z_c} = \frac{d - P}{\sqrt{PQ}} = \frac{-P}{\sqrt{PQ}}.$$ (5.5)

Equations (5.4) and (5.5) demonstrate that the discrete values of a two-category "latent class" factor are simple functions of the taxon base rate (P). They also suggest that factor analysis might be a useful tool for characterizing two-group mixture distributions with multiple indicators. This last point merits emphasis because it is rarely appreciated. On the contrary, we have heard from colleagues the mistaken belief that strong factor loadings are incompatible with taxonicity. In the next section, we will learn why that belief is demonstrably false: *Strong factor loadings neither refute nor corroborate taxonicity*. Only by considering the factor score distributions can we distinguish between the dimensional and latent class variants of the model.

Although Thurstone was familiar with Equations (5.4) and (5.5), he never developed these ideas further. Progress in this area had to wait until later investigators recognized the conceptual links between factor analysis and a related psychometric model called latent profile analysis.

Latent Profile Analysis and Factor Analysis

Latent profile analysis (LPA; Bartholomew, 1987; Gibson, 1959; Lazarsfeld, 1950) is a form of latent class analysis with real-valued observed variables and discrete-valued latent variables. Like all latent class models, latent profile analysis has a goal of finding the minimum number of latent classes that can accurately account for the covariation among the observed indicators (Clogg & Shockey, 1988; Molenaar & Von Eye, 1994).

The key parameters of LPA are the latent class sizes and, for each latent class, the *profile* of indicator means. Estimation of these parameters can be accomplished by either algebraic or maximum likelihood methods (Lazarsfeld & Henry, 1968; Takane, 1976). In either case, an assumption of the model is that, within each latent class, the correlations among the class indicators are precisely zero. In other words, the model assumes that *nuisance covariance is absent*[4] and that the model-implied correlations can

---

[4]More formally, the model assumes within-class mutual independence of the class indicators (i.e., local independence).

be expressed by the reduced form of the General Covariance Mixture Theorem (see Equation [3.9]).

Latent profile analysis and factor analysis are sometimes offered as distinct models for elucidating latent space. In these comparisons, LPA is characterized as a model for discrete latent variates (types, latent classes, taxa), whereas factor analysis is described as a model for continuous latent variates (traits, dimensions; although see comments by Thurstone in the previous section). Bartholomew (1987, pp. 36-37) has shown, however, that under some conditions the two models yield equivalent information. In particular, in two-group mixture distributions, LPA and factor analysis can generate identical (reproduced) covariance matrices for the taxon indicators. To understand Bartholomew's argument we need to consider the parameters of LPA in terms of the General Covariance Mixture Theorem.

We begin by examining the elements of the LPA loading matrix. Let $\bar{x}_{i(j)}$ and $\sigma^2_{i(j)}$ denote the mean and variance of indicator x_i for members of latent class j. Furthermore, let $\bar{\bar{x}}_i$ represent the grand mean of indicator x_i in the mixed sample and π_j the probability of membership in class j

$$(\sum_{j=1}^{2} \pi_j = 1).$$

When the latent profile model holds, it can be shown that these parameters are sufficient for describing the observed-variable covariance matrix from a two-group mixture distribution. Specifically,

$$\Sigma_{(x)} = \mathbf{LL'} + \mathbf{D}, \tag{5.6}$$

where

$$l_{ij} = \sqrt{\pi_j}\,(\bar{x}_{i(j)} - \bar{\bar{x}}_i)$$

and $\mathbf{D}$ is a diagonal matrix with diagonal elements equal to

$$\mathbf{D}_{(i,j)} = \sum_{j=1}^{2} \pi_j\,\sigma^2_{i(j)}.$$

   Notice the similarity between the matrix expressions for the latent
profile (Equation [5.6]) and factor analysis (Equation [5.3]) models. In
particular, notice that in both models the reproduced covariances are
calculated from the product of a loading matrix and its transpose. These
(loading) matrices are not equal, however. In LPA—for two-group
mixtures—$\mathbf{L}$ is a v (variables) $\times$ 2 (latent classes) matrix, whereas in factor
analysis Λ is a v (variables) $\times$ 1 (factor) matrix.[5] Although manifestly different, Bartholomew (1987, pp. 36-37) has shown how these matrices are
related. Specifically, Bartholomew notes that the ith row of $\mathbf{L}$ is given by

$$l_{i.} = \left[\sqrt{P}\, Q(\bar{x}_{i(t)} - \bar{x}_{i(c)}) \quad -\sqrt{Q}\, P(\bar{x}_{i(t)} - \bar{x}_{i(c)}) \right], \qquad (5.7)$$

whereas the ith row of Λ is given by

$$\lambda_i = \sqrt{PQ}\, (\bar{x}_{i(t)} - \bar{x}_{i(c)}), \qquad (5.8)$$

or when $\mathbf{X}$ contains standard scores:

$$\lambda_i = \lambda_{xf_z} = r_{xf_z} = \frac{(PQ)^{1/2}(\bar{x}_{i(t)} - \bar{x}_{i(c)})}{sd(x_i)} \qquad (5.9)$$

   The key point here is that, in both models, the elements of the loading
matrices are simple functions of the taxon base rate (P) and the within-
class indicator means ($\bar{x}_{i(t)}$ and $\bar{x}_{i(c)}$).

---

[5]Note that a factor analysis model cannot recover the loadings in $\mathbf{L}$ because the columns of
$\mathbf{L}$ are linearly dependent. For example, in a two-class LPA model, each row of $\mathbf{L}$ will sum
to zero when the column elements are weighted by the class base rates

$$\sqrt{P}\, l_{i,1} + \sqrt{Q}\, l_{i,2} \equiv 0.$$

Nevertheless, when the two-class LPA model holds, a factor pattern, Λ, exists such that

$$\Sigma_{(X)} = \Lambda\Lambda' + \Psi^2 = \mathbf{LL}' + \mathbf{D}.$$

These expressions are interesting but they are of little practical value without estimates of the taxonic parameters that define them. In the next section, we show how to estimate these parameters by means of a factor-score density plot.

Estimating the Parameters of the General Covariance Mixture Theorem With Factor Analysis

We begin by describing how to estimate the indicator means in the taxon and complement classes. To do so, perform a (common) factor analysis in the total (i.e., mixed) sample to obtain a standardized factor pattern matrix, Λ. Extract one factor so that Λ has order v (variables) $\times$ 1. Generalizing from Equations (5.4) and (5.5), it is easily demonstrated that, with standardized indicators, the profile of indicator means for the taxon class is given by

$$\Lambda \frac{Q}{\sqrt{PQ}},\qquad(5.10)$$

and the profile of means for the nontaxon class is given by

$$\Lambda \frac{-P}{\sqrt{PQ}}.\qquad(5.11)$$

A simple proof of (5.10) follows. Assume that λ_x equals a standardized factor loading for a single variable, x. Rewriting (5.8),

$$\lambda_x = (PQ)^{\frac{1}{2}}(\bar{x}_{t_z} - \bar{x}_{c_z}),\qquad(5.12)$$

so that

$$\lambda_x \frac{Q}{\sqrt{PQ}} = Q(\bar{x}_{t_z} - \bar{x}_{c_z}),\qquad(5.13)$$

and

$$Q(\bar{x}_{t_z} - \bar{x}_{c_t}) = (1 - P)(\bar{x}_{t_z} - \bar{x}_{c_z}),$$

$$= \bar{x}_{t_z} - P\bar{x}_{t_z} - \bar{x}_{c_z} + P\bar{x}_{c_z} .$$

$$(5.14)$$

Let $\bar{\bar{x}}$ denote the grand mean of x such that $\bar{\bar{x}} = P\bar{x}_{t_z} + Q\bar{x}_{c_z}$. Note that when x is standardized, $\bar{\bar{x}} = 0.00$ and $\bar{x}_{t_z} - \bar{\bar{x}} = \bar{x}_{t_z}$. Therefore,

$$\bar{x}_{t_z} - \bar{\bar{x}} = \bar{x}_{t_z} - (P\bar{x}_{t_z} + Q\bar{x}_{c_z}),$$

$$= \bar{x}_{t_z} - (P\bar{x}_{t_z} + (1 - P)\bar{x}_{c_z}),$$

$$= \bar{x}_{t_z} - P\bar{x}_{t_z} - \bar{x}_{c_z} + P\bar{x}_{c_z},$$

$$(5.15)$$

the above result being equivalent to Equation (5.14), which ends our proof. The proof of (5.11) follows similar logic.

To transform the profile of means to the raw score metric, multiply Equations (5.10) and (5.11) by the observed indicator standard deviations and add the observed indicator means.

L-Mode

L-Mode is the name of our factor-analytic procedure for estimating base rates and other taxonic parameters. We call the technique L-Mode because it estimates these parameters from the *latent modes* of a (1-factor) factor-score density plot. The method is based on Equations (5.4) and (5.5). Recall that in those equations we learned that true factor scores are simple functions of the base rate when the taxonic model holds. Some readers may question the utility of these results because they were taught that "true" factor scores are never observed and often poorly estimated (Tucker, 1971). While these points are true, they do not vitiate our objectives because L-Mode uses functions of the factor scores that are tightly constrained by the base rate.

Specifically, when the within-class distributions of the taxon indicators are symmetrical—not necessarily normal, and we really only require that they be *approximately* symmetrical because of the normalizing effect of the Central Limit Theorem—the estimated factor scores will form a bimodal distribution with modes centered at

$$\frac{Q}{\sqrt{PQ}} \text{ and } \frac{-P}{\sqrt{PQ}}.$$

This result assumes that the factor scores are unbiased. Popular methods for estimating factor scores do not meet this criterion,[6] although a method by Bartlett (1937) does provides unbiased estimates.[7] Bartlett's method factor scores are estimated by

$$(\Lambda'\Psi^{-2}\Lambda)^{-1}\Lambda'\Psi^{-2}z_i \tag{5.16}$$

where z_i represents a vector of standardized observed scores for individual i.

Once again, when the taxonic model holds the true factor scores (which correspond to the standardized dummy scores) will fall at

$$\frac{Q}{\sqrt{PQ}} \text{ and } \frac{-P}{\sqrt{PQ}}.$$

With dimensional data, however, the estimated scores will either have a single mode (often centered at 0.00) or multiple modes that are not derivable from the General Covariance Mixture Theorem. These points are graphically illustrated in Figure 5.1, which depicts L-Mode plots for example taxonic and nontaxonic data.

Notice that when data are generated in accord with a taxonic model, the factor-score density plots are "camel shaped," with two prominent humps, or modes. Equations (5.4) and (5.5) predict where these modes will occur, assuming that we know the taxon base rate. When the base rate is unknown we can use the observed modes to estimate the base rate. For example, letting $fs_{\text{U-Mode}}$ and $fs_{\text{L-Mode}}$ denote the factor scores that are associated with the upper and lower modes of the latent distribution, from previously described equations we have

---

[6]For example, Thurstone's (1935) widely used regression method generates biased estimates.
[7]In some statistical packages, Bartlett's (1937) method factor scores are called weighted least squares estimates.

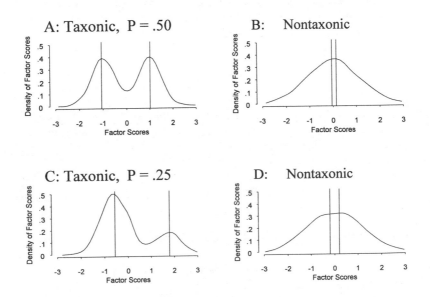

Figure 5.1.   Example L-Mode Plots for Taxonic and Nontaxonic Data

$$fs_{\text{U--Mode}} = \frac{Q}{\sqrt{PQ}}, \qquad (5.17)$$

$$P_U = \frac{1}{1 + fs_{\text{U--Mode}}^2} \qquad (5.18)$$

$$fs_{\text{L--Mode}} = \frac{-P}{\sqrt{PQ}}, \qquad (5.19)$$

and

$$P_L = 1 - \frac{1}{1 + fs_{\text{L--Mode}}^2}, \qquad (5.20)$$

Notice that the base rate estimates given by (5.18) and (5.20) are mathematically independent. In other words, L-Mode has a built-in consistency test. When these estimates agree *within a predefined tolerance limit* (this phrase is explicated in a later section), we have *prima facie* support for the taxonic conjecture. In some circumstances, the two estimates will be differentially biased, and one estimate is preferable to the other.

We can gauge the expected accuracy of the previous equations by considering their differentials. The question that concerns us here is the following: If one of the modes of the factor-score density plot is displaced from its theoretically specified position by an amount dx, how much bias (dP) is introduced in P_x (the corresponding estimate of the base rate)? A little calculus provides the answer. Letting a denote the upper mode of the density plot, from previous results,

$$P_U = \frac{1}{1 + a^2},$$ (5.21)

and the derivative of P with respect to a is

$$\frac{dP_U}{da} = \frac{-2a}{1 + 2a^2 + a^4}.$$ (5.22)

Then the differential of P with respect to a is given by

$$dP_U = \frac{-da\,2a}{1 + 2a^2 + a^4}.$$ (5.23)

Letting b denote the lower mode of the density plot,

$$P_L = 1 - \frac{1}{1 + b^2},$$ (5.24)

$$\frac{dP_L}{db} = \frac{2b}{1 + 2b^2 + b^4},$$ (5.25)

and

$$dP_L = \frac{db\,2b}{1 + 2b^2 + b^4}.$$ (5.26)

These results imply that when the base rate is less than .50, the upper mode, with its larger absolute value, has the smaller differential. Accordingly, we recommend that (1) when the two base rate estimates are close to .50, the average estimate should be used; (2) when P is smaller than .50, use the estimate from Equation (5.18); and (3) when P is larger than .50, use the estimate from Equation (5.20).

Figures 5.2 through 5.7 illustrate L-Mode plots for taxonic and nontaxonic samples with indicator correlations of .50, .43, and .26. For the taxonic samples, these values correspond to taxon base rates of .50, .25, and .10. Overall, the plots strongly support the usefulness of L-Mode for distinguishing taxonic from nontaxonic data. Notice in Figure 5.2, for instance, that when the true base rate equals .50, the modes of the factor-score density plots are very close to their theoretically derived values of −1.00 and +1.00. For the 25 samples depicted in Figure 5.2, the mean of the lower modes was −1.01, whereas the mean of the upper modes was .94. These numbers correspond to average base-rate estimates of .53 ($\sigma = .05$) and .50 ($\sigma = .07$), respectively. Although these estimates are slightly less precise and slightly more variable than those from MAXCOV-HITMAX or MAXEIG-HITMAX, they do provide an additional means of corroborating taxonic conjectures by offering an internal consistency test for the taxonic parameters. For instance, the mean absolute difference between the base rate estimates from the two modes was only .07 for the analyses depicted in Figure 5.2. For the nontaxonic samples depicted in Figure 5.3, the corresponding mean absolute difference was a whopping .90! In other · words, there was virtually no consistency between the two estimates in the nontaxonic data. We report findings for the remaining samples in the next section.

A Monte Carlo Comparison of L-Mode and Two Cluster Analysis Methods

In this section, we compare the classification capabilities of L-Mode and two widely used cluster analysis techniques: Ward's (1963) method (also called minimum variance, sum of squares, or the trace method) and Average Linkage (Sokal & Michener, 1958). Our Monte Carlo study used 350 samples of two-class taxonic data. These samples represent 25 data sets for each of 14 parameter configurations. The 350 samples were originally

(text continues on page 67)

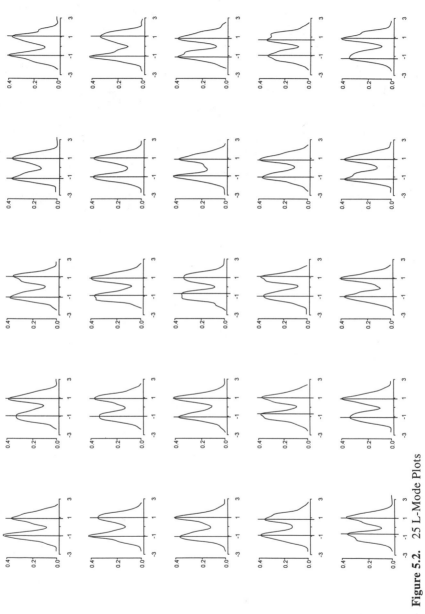

Figure 5.2. 25 L-Mode Plots

X-axis = factor scores; Y-axis = density of factor scores; $N = 600$; $P = .50$, 2.0 SD separation on each variable; no nuisance covariance, $r_{ij} = .50$ (because of complement-taxon mixture).

61

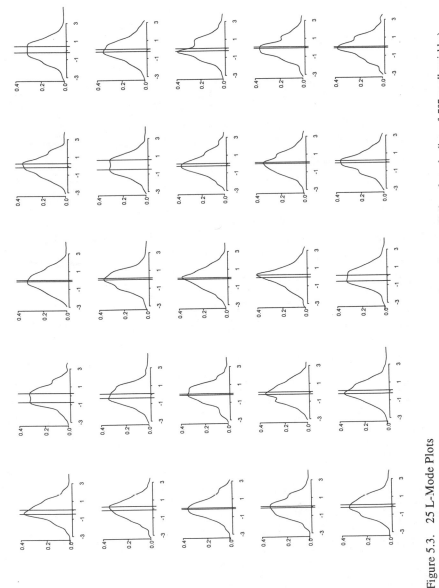

Figure 5.3.   25 L-Mode Plots

X-axis = factor scores; Y-axis = density of factor scores; N = 600; nontaxonic samples, r_{ij} = .50 (from factor loadings of .707 on all variables).

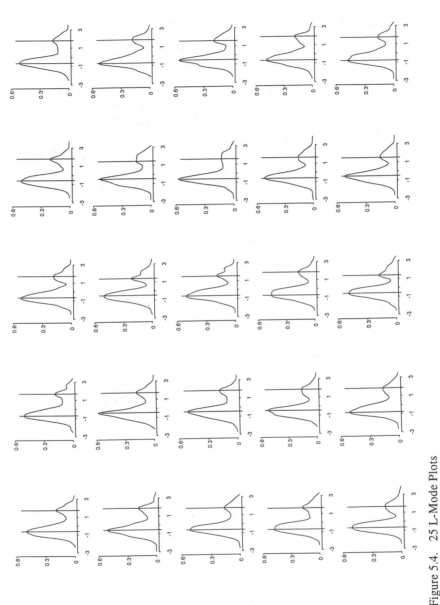

Figure 5.4.   25 L-Mode Plots

X-axis = factor scores; Y-axis = density of factor scores; N = 600; P = .25, 2.0 *SD* separation on each variable; no nuisance covariance, r_{ij} = .43 (because of complement-taxon mixture).

63

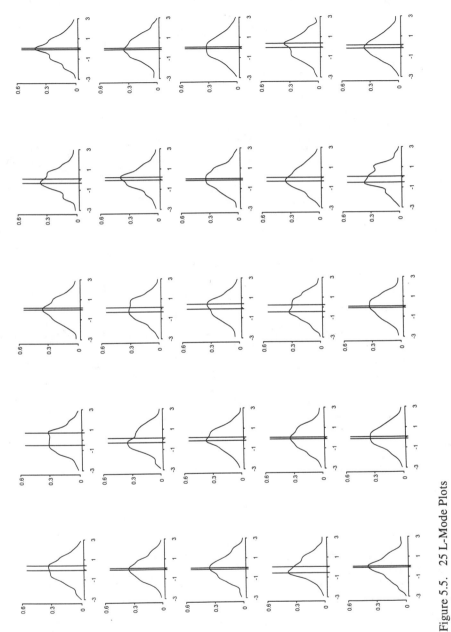

Figure 5.5.   25 L-Mode Plots

X-axis = factor scores; Y-axis = density of factor scores; $N = 600$; nontaxonic samples, $r_{ij} = .43$ (from factor loadings of .66 on all variables).

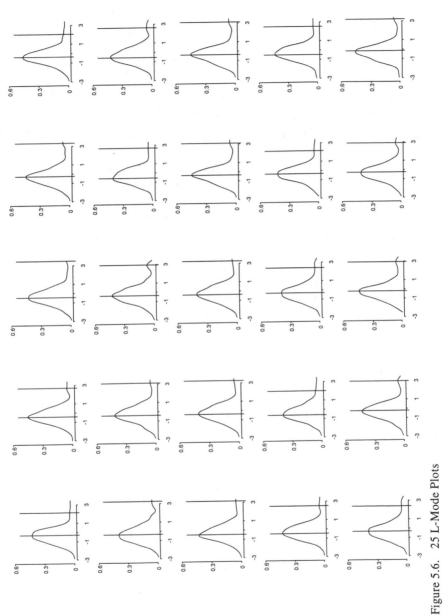

Figure 5.6.   25 L-Mode Plots

X-axis = factor scores; Y-axis = density of factor scores; N = 600; P = .10, 2.0 SD separation on each variable; no nuisance covariance, r_{ij} = .26 (because of complement-taxon mixture).

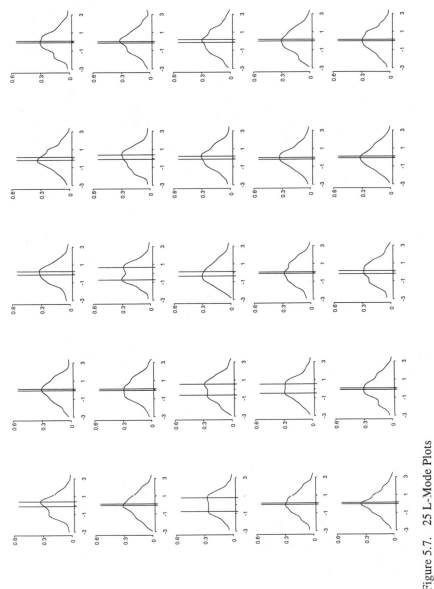

Figure 5.7.   25 L-Mode Plots

X-axis = factor scores; Y-axis = density of factor scores; N = 600; nontaxonic samples, r_{ij} = .26 (from factor loadings of .510 on all variables).

generated to evaluate other taxometric procedures (cf. Meehl & Yonce, 1994, 1996). They were used in the present study because they differ in (a) sample size, (b) base rates, (c) indicator validities (i.e., separation between the taxon and complement means), and (d) indicator covariation that is *not* due to the taxonic structure of the data (i.e., nuisance covariance from a common *dimensional* latent factor). All samples contain four continuously distributed variables with within-class Gaussian distributions. Identifying codes for the samples are reported in Table 5.1.

For the three classification methods, recovery accuracy was judged by two criteria. The first was the ability of each method to recover the known base rates in the various parameter configurations. Here, accuracy was indexed by calculating the base rate mean and standard deviation in the 25 trials of each cell of the design. For the cluster methods, base rates were calculated by selecting the last partition of the agglomerative hierarchy and identifying the cluster with the larger centroid (vector of means). This cluster was called the "taxon cluster." For each trial the proportion of total cases in the taxon cluster defined the trial base rate. In the L-Mode analyses four base rate estimates were calculated for each sample: (a) P_L; (c) P_U; (c) P_{avg}; and (d) P_{emp}. Using Equations (5.18) and (5.20), P_L and P_U were calculated from the lower and upper modes of the factor score distributions. The average of these estimates was called P_{avg}. We also estimated the base rate from the empirical classification assignments, P_{emp}. For these estimates, we first calculated the absolute distance between each factor score and the two scores that were below the factor-score modes. After comparing the distances, we assigned a subject to the closer of the two latent classes. All subjects were assigned to a latent class so that the L-Mode results would be directly comparable with the cluster analysis results.

As a second index of parameter recovery, we calculated the hit rate mean and standard deviation for each of the 14 parameter configurations. The observed "hit rate" was defined as the number of correct classification decisions in each sample (i.e., the sum of the true negative and true positive assignments divided by the total sample size). A summary of the base rate and hit rate results is reported in Table 5.2.

In this small simulation study, we found that P_{avg} provides more accurate and less variable estimates than either P_L or P_U in samples with equal numbers of taxon and complement members. This was especially true when the data contained sizable nuisance covariance (e.g., in samples N3-50-20 and N6-50-20). Notice, for example, that under these less than ideal conditions the lower and upper modes of the factor-score distributions were biased "outward" (i.e., too high and too low, respectively) from

TABLE 5.1 Parameter Configurations for Monte Carlo Samples

			Taxonic Configuration		
N^a	P^b	SD^c	Factor Loadings[d]	File Code[e]	Expected r_{ij}^f
100	.50	2.0	0	A1-50-20	.50
200	.50	2.0	0	A2-50-20	.50
300	.50	2.0	0	A3-50-20	.50
600	.50	2.0	0	A6-50-20	.50
300	.25	2.0	0	A3-25-20	.43
600	.25	2.0	0	A6-25-20	.43
300	.10	2.0	0	A3-10-20	.26
600	.10	2.0	0	A6-10-20	.26
300	.50	1.5	0	A3-50-15	.36
600	.50	1.5	0	A6-50-15	.36
300	.50	2.0	$x = .70$ $y = .50$ $z = .40$ $v = .20$	N3-50-20	$r_{xy} = .68\ r_{yz} = .60$ $r_{xz} = .64\ r_{yv} = .55$ $r_{xv} = .57\ r_{zv} = .54$
600	.50	2.0	Same as for N3-50-20	N6-50-20	Same as for N3-50-20
300	.50	$x = 2.00$ $y = 1.75$ $z = 1.50$ $v = 1.25$	$x = .70$ $y = .50$ $z = .40$ $v = .20$	D3-50-v1	$r_{xy} = .65\ r_{yz} = .52$ $r_{xz} = .58\ r_{yv} = .41$ $r_{xv} = .46\ r_{zv} = .37$
600	.50	Same as for D3-50-v1	Same as for D3-50-v1	D6-50-v1	Same as for D3-50-v1

a. Sample size.
b. Base rate.
c. Amount of separation, same for all four variables unless given otherwise.
d. Same for all variables in taxon and in complement groups unless given otherwise.
e. Filename coding used by the authors for identification of the Monte Carlo samples.
f. Same for all variables unless given otherwise.

their theoretically predicted values. Averaging these estimates, however, largely corrected this bias.

A second noteworthy finding from these analyses is that when the true base rate was .50, the empirically derived estimates from L-Mode (P_{emp}) were often two to three times less variable than the corresponding Ward's

TABLE 5.2 Summary of Monte Carlo Comparisons of L-Mode and Two Cluster Analysis Methods

Base-Rate Estimates

	P = .50										P = .25		P = .10	
	A1-50-20	A2-50-20	A3-50-20	A6-50-20	A3-50-15	A6-50-15	N3-50-20	N6-50-20	D3-50-v1	D6-50-v1	A3-25-20	A6-25-20	A3-10-20	A6-10-20
L-Mode P_1	.53 (.09)	.51 (.08)	.50 (.05)	.53 (.06)	.49 (.10)	.53 (.08)	.59 (.12)	.58 (.07)	.61 (.10)	.63 (.11)	.25 (.05)	.26 (.04)	.11 (.03)	.11 (.03)
L-Mode P_2	.46 (.12)	.50 (.07)	.47 (.05)	.50 (.07)	.44 (.15)	.52 (.08)	.43 (.12)	.43 (.08)	.44 (.11)	.38 (.10)	.29 (.10)	.26 (.07)	.12 (.11)	.12 (.07)
L-Mode P_{avg}	.50 (.08)	.50 (.04)	.49 (.03)	.51 (.05)	.47 (.08)	.52 (.05)	.51 (.09)	.50 (.05)	.52 (.07)	.50 (.08)	.27 (.05)	.26 (.03)	.11 (.06)	.12 (.04)
L-Mode P_{emp}	.49 (.03)	.50 (.02)	.50 (.01)	.51 (.01)	.49 (.04)	.51 (.02)	.51 (.04)	.50 (.02)	.51 (.03)	.50 (.04)	.27 (.02)	.27 (.01)	.13 (.03)	.13 (.02)
Ward's	.48 (.09)	.49 (.08)	.48 (.04)	.51 (.02)	.50 (.09)	.52 (.06)	.49 (.10)	.51 (.08)	.53 (.12)	.50 (.09)	.27 (.06)	.25 (.03)	.14 (.10)	.11 (.03)
Average Linkage	.46 (.20)	.47 (.10)	.51 (.14)	.38 (.26)	.33 (.35)	.42 (.42)	.39 (.30)	.44 (.30)	.31 (.26)	.52 (.37)	.30 (.28)	.31 (.21)	.13 (.18)	.09 (.04)

Hit-Rate Estimates

	A1-50-20	A2-50-20	A3-50-20	A6-50-20	A3-50-15	A6-50-15	N3-50-20	N6-50-20	D3-50-v1	D6-50-v1	A3-25-20	A6-25-20	A3-10-20	A6-10-20
L-Mode	.97 (.02)	.97 (.01)	.98 (.01)	.98 (.01)	.92 (.02)	.93 (.01)	.93 (.02)	.93 (.01)	.93 (.01)	.90 (.02)	.97 (.01)	.97 (.01)	.97 (.03)	.97 (.02)
Ward's	.93 (.07)	.94 (.06)	.95 (.03)	.96 (.01)	.88 (.05)	.89 (.02)	.89 (.05)	.91 (.05)	.85 (.04)	.87 (.03)	.95 (.04)	.96 (.01)	.95 (.10)	.97 (.03)
Average Linkage	.89 (.17)	.95 (.09)	.92 (.13)	.81 (.22)	.66 (.20)	.62 (.19)	.75 (.21)	.77 (.20)	.72 (.18)	.68 (.19)	.84 (.24)	.91 (.20)	.94 (.18)	.97 (.03)

estimates and as much as 10 to 20 times less variable than the Average Linkage estimates. In other words, besides providing a graphical means of evaluating taxonic conjectures, L-Mode seems to provide better taxon assignments than either of the two cluster methods that were used in our study. We find a similar picture painted by the hit rate summaries in the bottom half of Table 5.2.

Notice, for example, that L-Mode produced the highest average hit rates across the 14 conditions of our design (in one parameter configuration, L-Mode tied with Ward's method). The taxometric results were also less variable than those from the cluster algorithms. This was especially true for the L-Mode/Average Linkage comparisons and to a lesser extent for the L-Mode/Ward comparisons. Interestingly, Ward's method often performed well in situations where Average Linkage performed dismally (e.g., see conditions A3-50-15 and A6-50-15). This finding diverges from those of earlier cluster comparison work (Blashfield & Aldenderfer, 1988) although it is consistent with more recent findings (Waller, Kaiser, Illian, & Manry, in press).

Although the scope of this study is admittedly limited, we believe our results provide ample support for the following conclusion: *L-Mode generates taxometric parameter estimates that are less biased and more efficient than those from Ward's method or Average Linkage* (two of the most widely used cluster methods in the behavioral and life sciences). Perhaps our findings should come as no surprise. Of the three classification schemes, L-Mode is the only algorithm based on a model of cluster formation (i.e., the General Covariance Mixture Theorem). Ward's method and Average Linkage—like most cluster algorithms—define cluster membership on the basis of an arbitrarily defined similarity measure and an atheoretical minimization function.[8] With L-Mode, *the taxometric model of cluster recovery is derivable from the taxometric model of cluster formation.*

An important property of L-Mode is that the observed data and the factor scores are on *qualitatively* different metrics. In the metric of the observed data, for instance, the distance between the complement and taxon indicator means (i.e., the indicator validities) can realize any positive value. This is not true with the factor scores. As we saw earlier in the chapter, the distance between the factor score modes is a function of the taxon base rate, and the strength of the indicator validities is captured by the factor loadings (see Equation [5.9]). Table 5.3 reports the values of the predicted

---

[8]These cluster methods can even generate different solutions by simply reordering the rows of the data matrix (see Blashfield & Aldenderfer, 1988, p. 450).

TABLE 5.3 Lower and Upper Factor Score Modes for Various Base Rates

Base Rate (P)	Lower Mode	Upper Mode	Intermode Distance
0.10	−0.33	3.00	3.33
0.15	−0.42	2.38	2.80
0.20	−0.50	2.00	2.50
0.25	−0.58	1.73	2.31
0.30	−0.65	1.53	2.18
0.35	−0.73	1.36	2.10
0.40	−0.82	1.22	2.04
0.45	−0.90	1.11	2.01
0.50	−1.00	1.00	2.00
0.55	−1.11	0.90	2.01
0.60	−1.22	0.82	2.04
0.65	−1.36	0.73	2.10
0.70	−1.53	0.65	2.18
0.75	−1.73	0.58	2.31
0.80	−2.00	0.50	2.50
0.85	−2.38	0.42	2.80
0.90	−3.00	0.33	3.33

modes and the intermode distances for a sample of base rates between .10 and .90.

This table shows that the minimum distance between the factor score modes should occur when $P = .50$. It also shows that when the base rate diverges toward the closed boundary points of the [0, 1] probability interval the intermode distance increases. This suggests that L-Mode plots will be less well defined when the base rate is close to .50 and the indicator validities are low (because of the increased scatter around the modal values). All things considered, weak indicators should produce overlapping, platykurtic factor-score distributions, whereas strong indicators should produce well separated leptokurtic distributions. Although this statement is correct, it is also incomplete because it ignores the influence of indicator number. That is, as the number of indicators rises, the characteristic shape of a taxonic L-Mode plot should become increasingly apparent.

Figure 5.8 illustrates the important point of the last paragraph. The first panel in the figure shows a histogram of two normal distributions that are separated by one within-class standard deviation. Clearly, the taxonic

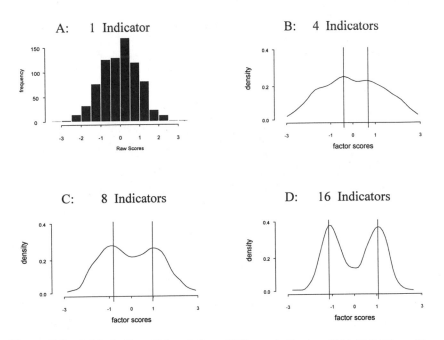

Figure 5.8.   L-Mode Plots Using 4, 8, or 16 Taxon Indicators With Validities of 1 σ Separation

status of these data is impossible to detect with the unaided eye. Notice, for instance, the absence of any compelling signs of bimodality. You may recall from Chapter 2 that a univariate mixture of two normal distributions will generally not reveal bimodality unless the taxon and complement means are separated by two or more within-class standard deviations (Murphy, 1964; Robertson & Fryer, 1969; Roeder, 1994). This is perhaps the best reason for using multivariate techniques in taxometric research. As illustrated in the remaining panels of Figure 5.8, bimodality is easily discerned when the variables are optimally weighted, pooled, and expressed in the metric of the factor scores—in other words, when we have performed an L-Mode analysis (we saw similar results with the MAXEIG-HITMAX technique).

Factor-Analytic Techniques for
Distinguishing Types From Continua:
Q-Factor Analysis

People come in four types, the pomegranate (hard on the outside, hard on the inside), the walnut (hard-soft), the prune (soft-hard), and the grape (soft-soft).

—Muhammad Ali

In the preceding chapter we learned that factor analysis can be used to estimate taxonic parameters in two-group mixture distributions. In this chapter, we consider an alternative factor model for finding groups in data. This model is called Q-factor analysis (Burt, 1912, 1917, 1940; Stephenson, 1936a, 1936b), and although it does not belong to the family of procedures that we have discussed so far, there are several compelling reasons for reviewing Q-factor analysis in this book. One reason is that it continues to be used for classification purposes in the social (Arffa, Fitzhugh-Bell, & Black, 1989; York & John, 1992) and physical (Imbrie & Purdy, 1962) sciences,[1] although its suitability for this task has been questioned for decades (Block, 1955; Cattell, 1952; Cronbach & Gleser, 1953; Eysenck, 1954; Fleiss, Lawlor, Platman, & Fieve, 1971). Another is our desire to show that Q-factor analysis—as it is typically applied in the social sciences (Block, 1971; Robins, John, Caspi, Moffit, & Stouthamer-Loeber, 1996; York & John, 1992)—cannot identify the "type" of taxa discussed in preceding chapters. We also want to show that Q-factor analysis and L-Mode *can* yield functionally equivalent results when appropriate distance measures (Cronbach & Gleser, 1953; Nunnally, 1962; Osgood & Suci, 1952) are used to index profile similarity. To accomplish

---

[1]Brown (1968) has written a comprehensive review of the literature through 1968.

these goals, we have organized this chapter into four main sections. In the first two sections, we review the mathematics of L-Mode and Q-factor analysis and then compare and contrast these methods by applying them to a common data set. We next consider the various ways in which profile similarity can be measured and critically evaluate the use of Q correlations for clustering profiles into homogeneous groups. In the final section, we describe the conditions under which Q-factor analysis can identify taxa that are consistent with the General Covariance Mixture Theorem. Before discussing these topics, we describe the data set used in our examples.

The Example Data Set

To illustrate the techniques discussed in this chapter, we have selected a subset of data from a recent taxometric study of dissociative experiences (Waller, Putnam, & Carlson, 1996). Psychological dissociation is one of the most widely studied and controversial topics (Cohen, Berzoff, & Elin, 1995; North, Ryall, Ricci, & Wetzel, 1993) in the field of psychopathology, and in a book on taxometrics we obviously cannot cover this topic in any detail. Nevertheless, we can provide some essential information that should animate the numbers of our illustrations.

Dissociation is commonly defined as "a disruption in the usually integrated functions of consciousness, memory, identity, or perception of the environment" (American Psychiatric Association, 1994, p. 447). Individuals with extreme dissociative symptoms may suffer from a dissociative disorder. The most common symptoms of these disorders are amnesia for dissociative states (e.g., finding oneself in a place and having no idea how you got there), depersonalization (e.g., feeling that your body does not belong to you), and feelings of derealization (e.g., feeling that the world is not real).

There are many interesting questions about dissociation and the dissociative disorders that have yet to be resolved (for a review, see Lynn & Rhue, 1994), but from the perspective of this chapter, one of the most intriguing questions is whether or not dissociation is a taxonic variable. The currently popular view is that dissociative experiences exist along a continuum of severity and that persons with extreme scores on this continuum qualify for a dissociative disorder. This represents a dimensional model of dissociation. An alternative model, one that was first proposed more than a century ago by the French psychiatrist Pierre Janet (1889), holds that only a small class of individuals are vulnerable to dissociative states. According to this view, most individuals never experience pathological dissociation. Janet's theory represents a taxonic model of dissociation.

The two models described above provide an ideal problem for a taxometric analysis. Attempting to resolve this problem, Waller, Putnam, and Carlson (1996) recently applied three taxometric procedures—MAXCOV (Meehl, 1973a; Meehl & Yonce, 1996), MAMBAC (Meehl & Yonce, 1994), and MAXSLOPE (Grove & Meehl, 1993)—to dissociative symptom data from 228 individuals with diagnosed dissociative identity disorder and to 228 normal controls. The dissociative symptoms were measured by the widely used Dissociative Experiences Scale (DES; Bernstein-Carlson & Putnam, 1986).

The results of the Waller, Putnam, and Carlson (1996) study strongly corroborated the taxonic model of dissociation. Additionally, the authors identified eight DES items that maximally discriminated dissociative taxon members from nontaxon members. These items were combined into a scale they labeled the DES-T.

In the examples presented below, we use DES-T data from six individuals who were part of the Waller, Putnam, et al. (1996) study. Three of them have been diagnosed with dissociative identity disorder, whereas the other three have no known psychological problems. Because many readers will be unfamiliar with dissociation in general, and the DES-T in particular, we report the eight items (labeled D1 through D8) of the DES-T in Table 6.1.[2]

The raw data for our examples are reported below in the matrix labeled **X**. Each row of **X** contains the item response profile for one subject (S). The first three profiles come from individuals diagnosed with dissociative identity disorder.

$$
\mathbf{X} =
\begin{array}{c}
\\
S1 \\ S2 \\ S3 \\ S4 \\ S5 \\ S6
\end{array}
\begin{array}{cccccccc}
D1 & D2 & D3 & D4 & D5 & D6 & D7 & D8 \\
80 & 50 & 90 & 65 & 75 & 85 & 100 & 100 \\
80 & 15 & 95 & 75 & 100 & 100 & 100 & 80 \\
85 & 90 & 90 & 70 & 80 & 90 & 85 & 95 \\
10 & 0 & 0 & 0 & 0 & 10 & 10 & 0 \\
10 & 0 & 0 & 10 & 20 & 0 & 0 & 0 \\
0 & 0 & 20 & 0 & 0 & 0 & 15 & 0
\end{array}
.
$$

A useful feature of these data is that the taxonic structure of **X** is clearly visible to the naked eye. The numbers in rows 1-3 are noticeably larger than those in the remaining rows. Obviously, most data sets are not as

---

[2]Scores on the DES-T items theoretically range from 0 to 100 (in 5-point increments), with higher numbers denoting increasing symptom severity.

TABLE 6.1 The DES-T

D1   Some people have the experience of finding themselves in a place and having no idea how they got there.

D2   Some people have the experience of finding new things among their belongings that they do not remember buying.

D3   Some people sometimes have the experience of feeling as though they are standing next to themselves or watching themselves do something, and they actually see themselves as if they were looking at another person.

D4   Some people are told that they sometimes do not recognize friends or family members.

D5   Some people have the experience of feeling that other people, objects, and the world around them are not real.

D6   Some people have the experience of feeling that their body does not seem to belong to them.

D7   Some people find that in one situation they may act so differently compared with another situation that they feel almost as if they were two different people.

D8   Some people sometimes find that they hear voices inside their head that tell them to do things or comment on things that they are doing.

---

clearly structured, and the researcher would be well advised to supplement "interocular cluster analysis" with a newer and more reliable taxometric procedure, such as L-Mode.

An L-Mode Analysis of the Dissociation Data

You may recall from Chapter 5 that there are four major components of an L-Mode analysis. First, the correlations among the putative taxon indicators arc factor analyzed by classical factor methods. Second, Bartlett-method factor scores are computed for the first unrotated factor. Third, the estimated scores are used to compute a nonparametric estimate of the factor-score probability density (Silverman, 1986; Wegman, 1972), and lastly, the modes of the density are located and used to calculate two estimates of the taxon base rate (using Equations [5.18] and [5.20]). If the independent estimates yield mutually corroborative support for the taxonic hypothesis, then the factor scores can also be used to assign individuals to the latent classes.

For many reasons, L-Mode is easier to describe than it is to illustrate. For instance, the computations that are involved in a factor analysis are iterative by nature, and the calculations that are required to compute a nonparametric density estimate can be daunting. Fortunately, we can achieve the goals of this chapter—without getting bogged down in the math—by substituting a principal components analysis (and component scores) for the factor analysis (and factor scores). Additionally, by restricting our example to six cases we can work directly with the estimated factor scores[3] rather than with the factor-score density.

Let X_z denote the matrix of standard scores that is formed by scaling X to have column means of 0.00 and standard deviations of 1.00.

	D1	D2	D3	D4	D5	D6	D7	D8
S1	.868	.654	.866	.769	.658	.769	1.006	1.070
S2	.868	-.293	.972	1.041	1.222	1.077	1.006	.675
S3	.989	1.737	.866	.905	.771	.872	.694	.971
S4	-.828	-.699	-1.043	-.995	-1.034	-.769	-.868	-.905
S5	-.828	-.699	-1.043	-.724	-.583	-.974	-1.076	-.905
S6	-1.070	-.699	-.618	-.995	-1.034	-.974	-.763	-.905

$X_z =$ (above matrix).

Notice that by standardizing *within columns* we did not distort the relative distances between the column elements, and we find that the taxonic structure of X is easily seen in X_z. To compute the correlations among the DES-T items, we take

$$R_X = X_z' X_z \frac{1}{N-1}.$$

This yields

	D1	D2	D3	D4	D5	D6	D7	D8
D1	1.000	.788	.968	.991	.968	.990	.972	.988
D2		1.000	.735	.734	.653	.720	.692	.818
D3			1.000	.974	.950	.977	.990	.974
D4				1.000	.991	.988	.970	.972
D5					1.000	.973	.948	.935
D6						1.000	.984	.971
D7							1.000	.976
D8								1.000

$R_X =$ (above matrix).

[3]In the remainder of this section we continue to use the terms "factor analysis" and "factor scores" even though we are working with "components analysis" and "components scores."

The interitem correlations in this example are unusually high because (a) the taxon base rate is .50 by design, (b) the item variances are unusually small in the nontaxon class, and (c) the item means in the taxon and non-taxon classes (the latent validities) are far apart (Waller, Putnam, & Carlson, 1996). Using well-known theory (Green, 1978, p. 353), these correlations can be decomposed into a triple product of eigenvectors and eigenvalues such that

$$\mathbf{R_X} = \mathbf{ULU'}, \tag{6.1}$$

where $\mathbf{U}$ is a matrix of eigenvectors and $\mathbf{L}$ is a diagonal matrix of eigenvalues (characteristic roots). From these matrices, the matrix of factor loadings, Λ, is given by

$$\Lambda = \mathbf{UL}^{\frac{1}{2}}. \tag{6.2}$$

For the example data,[4]

$$
\mathbf{U} = \begin{bmatrix}
.365 & .005 & .174 & -.450 & -.018 & .495 & .602 & -.159 \\
.289 & .912 & .099 & .139 & -.121 & -.159 & -.013 & -.124 \\
.361 & -.099 & -.425 & .681 & -.111 & .298 & .232 & .246 \\
.364 & -.124 & .328 & .141 & .131 & .451 & -.652 & -.281 \\
.355 & -.278 & .590 & .285 & .168 & -.515 & .268 & .041 \\
.363 & -.147 & .013 & -.305 & -.728 & -.159 & -.245 & .371 \\
.360 & -.187 & -.516 & -.132 & .027 & -.372 & -.027 & -.642 \\
.364 & .096 & -.239 & -.319 & .630 & -.089 & -.162 & .519
\end{bmatrix},
$$

$$Diag(\mathbf{L}) = [7.431 \quad 0.453 \quad 0.078 \quad 0.024 \quad 0.014 \quad 0.000 \quad 0.000 \quad 0.000],$$

and

$$
\Lambda_1 = \begin{array}{c} D1 \\ D2 \\ D3 \\ D4 \\ D5 \\ D6 \\ D7 \\ D8 \end{array}
\begin{bmatrix} .996 \\ .789 \\ .985 \\ .992 \\ .967 \\ .990 \\ .981 \\ .992 \end{bmatrix}
=
\begin{bmatrix} .367 \\ .289 \\ .361 \\ .364 \\ .355 \\ .363 \\ .360 \\ .364 \end{bmatrix} \times \sqrt{7.43}.
$$

with column headings $\Lambda_1 \quad \mathbf{U}_1 \quad \mathbf{L}_1^{\frac{1}{2}}$

___

[4]The values in columns 6-8 of $\mathbf{U}$ may vary across matrix algebra programs or computing platforms. The rank of $\mathbf{R_X}$ is less than its order (because we have fewer subjects than variables) and some eigenvalues of $\mathbf{L}$ equal 0.00. The corresponding eigenvectors (columns

We are now well positioned to test the taxonic hypothesis by computing factor scores and noting whether the score modes occur at their predicted values. Recall that our example includes three taxon members and three nontaxon members; thus the taxon base rate for **X** is .50. Referring back to Table 5.3, we find that when the base rate equals .50 the predicted values for the factor-score modes equal −1.00 and +1.00.

There are several reasons why we do not expect the observed modes to fall *exactly* at their predicted values. One reason is that we are working with component scores rather than unbiased factor scores (such as Bartlett factor scores). Another is that self-reported symptom data generally have *some* nuisance covariance—often due to response sets—and thus the indicator correlation matrices in the taxon and complement classes will generally not equal identity matrices. Finally, we are unlikely to find *any* modes with only six factor scores.

What we do find, in fact, is that the *average* factor scores (ξ) for the taxon and nontaxon members are reasonably close to their predicted values (+1.00 and −1.00).

$$\xi = \mathbf{X}_z \cdot \mathbf{U}_1 \mathbf{\Lambda}_1^{-\frac{1}{2}} = \begin{matrix} S1 & S2 & S3 & S4 & S5 & S6 \\ [\,.867 & .878 & .990 & -.929 & -.889 & -.919\,]. \end{matrix}$$

The averages for Subjects 1-3 and 4-6 equal .91 and −.91, respectively. It is interesting, and not a coincidence, that both averages are biased by the same amount (.09). The most interesting feature of these scores, however, is that they clearly illuminate the taxonic structure of the original data. That is, L-Mode has correctly identified the two-group structure of the dissociation item-response arrays. Let us now consider how Q-factor analysis fares in this case.

A Q-Factor Analysis of the Dissociation Data

Q-factor analysis is an old method for clustering profiles (Burt, 1912, 1917). The heyday of Q-factor research occurred during the 1930s and 1940s (Burt, 1940; Burt & Stephenson, 1939; Stephenson, 1935, 1936a, 1936b), although in certain areas of psychology the technique is still

---

6-8 of **U**) of the 0.00 eigenvalues are not uniquely determined. One way of understanding this is to note that $\mathbf{R_X}$ will equal **ULU′** regardless of what values are in the last three columns of **U**.

widely used. For instance, in personality research, Q-factor analysis has recently been used to identity *ideal types* or prototypical configurations of personality trait scores (Robins et al., 1996; York & John, 1992). Typically in this research, Q-factor analysis is used to summarize the underlying structure of a matrix of Q correlations. Thus, to fully understand Q-factor analysis as it is often applied, we need to understand the nature of a Q correlation.

A Q correlation is simply a Pearson product moment correlation between subject arrays or trait profiles (rather than variable arrays[5]). Mathematically, there is nothing remarkable about how Q correlations work. They can be computed using standard software by simply transposing a persons × variables matrix into a variables × persons matrix prior to calculating the correlations.

To illustrate Q-factor analysis, we use this technique to summarize the Q correlations from the example dissociation data. Our goal here is to identify the Q-factors—or "ideal types"—that correspond to pathological dissociators and nondissociators. Following standard practice (Burt & Stephenson, 1939), we compute the Q correlations from a variable-standardized matrix.

Let $\mathbf{X}^*$ denote the transpose of $\mathbf{X}_z$ (computed in the previous section) such that

$$\mathbf{X}^* = \mathbf{X}_z' = \begin{array}{c} \\ D1 \\ D2 \\ D3 \\ D4 \\ D5 \\ D6 \\ D7 \\ D8 \end{array} \begin{array}{cccccc} S1 & S2 & S3 & S4 & S5 & S6 \\ \left[\begin{array}{cccccc} .868 & 868 & .989 & -.828 & -.828 & -1.070 \\ .654 & -.293 & 1.737 & -.699 & -.699 & -.699 \\ .866 & .972 & .866 & -1.043 & -1.043 & -.618 \\ .769 & 1.041 & .905 & -.995 & -.724 & -.995 \\ .658 & 1.222 & .771 & -1.034 & -.583 & -1.034 \\ .769 & 1.077 & .872 & -.769 & -.974 & -.974 \\ 1.006 & 1.006 & .694 & -.868 & -1.076 & -.763 \\ 1.070 & .675 & .971 & -.905 & -.905 & -.905 \end{array} \right] \end{array}.$$

After scaling this matrix so that each column has a mean of 0.00 and a standard deviation of 1.00, we have

---

[5]For this reason, Q-factor analysis is often called inverse factor analysis (Stephenson, 1936b) or obverse factor analysis (Cattell, 1952).

$$\mathbf{X}_z^* = \begin{array}{c} \\ D1 \\ D2 \\ D3 \\ D4 \\ D5 \\ D6 \\ D7 \\ D8 \end{array} \begin{array}{c} S1 \\ \begin{bmatrix} .235 \\ -1.183 \\ .221 \\ -.420 \\ -1.157 \\ -.421 \\ 1.153 \\ 1.573 \end{bmatrix} \end{array} \begin{array}{c} S2 \\ .099 \\ -2.333 \\ .316 \\ .460 \\ .840 \\ .536 \\ .388 \\ -.306 \end{array} \begin{array}{c} S3 \\ .042 \\ 2.360 \\ -.340 \\ -.219 \\ -.634 \\ -.322 \\ -.872 \\ -.014 \end{array} \begin{array}{c} S4 \\ .517 \\ 1.536 \\ -1.192 \\ -.818 \\ -1.126 \\ .983 \\ .199 \\ -.099 \end{array} \begin{array}{c} S5 \\ .149 \\ .878 \\ -1.072 \\ .739 \\ 1.540 \\ -.683 \\ -1.261 \\ -.291 \end{array} \begin{array}{c} S6 \\ -1.116 \\ 1.091 \\ 1.573 \\ -.673 \\ -.904 \\ -.546 \\ .709 \\ -.135 \end{bmatrix} \end{array}.$$

If you look closely at these matrices you will notice that something important distinguishes $\mathbf{X}^*$ from $\mathbf{X}_z^*$. Specifically, when we standardized the subject arrays of $\mathbf{X}^*$ we effectively removed all signs of taxonicity from the data. That is, when looking at $\mathbf{X}_z^*$, it is difficult to see that Subjects 1-3 and 4-6 belong to different latent classes. This result may surprise some contemporary users of Q-factor analysis, although it would not have surprised many of the early users. For instance, William Stephenson (1952), who was one of the developers and most vociferous advocates of this technique, maintained that Q-factor analysis should only be used when "all important information for each [person] array is contained in its variation (no information is contained in the variate means)" (p. 485). Curiously, some influential users of factor analysis have not always recognized this important point. For instance, Cattell (1952) once claimed that "Q technique has its chief use as a classificatory device for finding the subpopulations in a nonhomogeneous population *like Lazarsfeld's 'latent structure analysis' or latent subgroup analysis*" (p. 502, emphasis added). However, as we saw in Chapter 5, Lazarsfeld's (1950) techniques, like our own, were developed to identify taxa that are consistent with the General Covariance Mixture Theorem.

Although it is difficult for us to *see* signs of taxonicity in the previous matrix, perhaps Q-factor analysis has keener eyesight. To find out, we must compute the Q correlations from $\mathbf{X}_z^*$. Doing so yields

$$\mathbf{R}_{X^*} = \begin{array}{c} \\ S1 \\ S2 \\ S3 \\ S4 \\ S5 \\ S6 \end{array} \begin{array}{c} S1 \\ \begin{bmatrix} 1.000 \\ \\ \\ \\ \\ \end{bmatrix} \end{array} \begin{array}{c} S2 \\ .204 \\ 1.000 \\ \\ \\ \\ \end{array} \begin{array}{c} S3 \\ -.418 \\ -.964 \\ 1.000 \\ \\ \\ \end{array} \begin{array}{c} S4 \\ -.093 \\ -.657 \\ .637 \\ 1.000 \\ \\ \end{array} \begin{array}{c} S5 \\ -.708 \\ -.215 \\ .375 \\ -.075 \\ 1.000 \\ \end{array} \begin{array}{c} S6 \\ .137 \\ -.457 \\ .324 \\ .058 \\ -.467 \\ 1.000 \end{bmatrix} \end{array},$$

which can be decomposed into $R_X^* = U^* L^* U^{*'}$ such that

$$
U^* = \begin{bmatrix}
-.295 & -.501 & .311 & -.705 & .127 & .230 \\
-.560 & .186 & .031 & .341 & -.066 & .728 \\
.584 & -.035 & -.042 & -.189 & -.614 & .492 \\
.414 & -.197 & .667 & .394 & .392 & .192 \\
.238 & .630 & -.113 & -.412 & .540 & .268 \\
.174 & -.527 & -.666 & .163 & .396 & .256
\end{bmatrix},
$$

and

$$
Diag(L^*) = [2.834 \quad 1.893 \quad 0.840 \quad 0.396 \quad 0.037 \quad 0.000].
$$

Using these results we find that the Q-factor loadings are given by

$$
\begin{array}{c}
\Lambda^* \\
\end{array}
\qquad
\begin{array}{c}
U^* \\
\end{array}
\qquad
\begin{array}{c}
L^{*\frac{1}{2}} \\
\end{array}
$$

$$
\Lambda^* = \begin{array}{c}
S1 \\ S2 \\ S3 \\ S4 \\ S5 \\ S6
\end{array}
\begin{bmatrix}
-.497 & -.689 \\
-.942 & .257 \\
.984 & -.048 \\
.697 & -.271 \\
.401 & .866 \\
.292 & -.725
\end{bmatrix}
=
\begin{bmatrix}
-.295 & -.501 \\
-.560 & .187 \\
.584 & -.035 \\
.414 & -.197 \\
.238 & .630 \\
.174 & -.527
\end{bmatrix}
\cdot
\begin{bmatrix}
\sqrt{2.834} & 0 \\
0 & \sqrt{1.893}
\end{bmatrix}.
$$

What have we learned here? The most important finding of this example is that the factor loadings from the Q correlations provide no evidence that the six subjects come from two distinct groups. In other words, there is no rotation for Λ^* such that Subjects 1-3 and 4-6 have high loadings on separate factors. For instance, the Varimax rotated loadings shown below clearly provide no support for the taxonic hypothesis:

$$
\text{Varimax-rotated } \Lambda^* = \begin{bmatrix}
-.235 & -.816 \\
-.973 & -.076 \\
.942 & .287 \\
.748 & -.020 \\
.085 & .951 \\
.520 & -.584
\end{bmatrix}.
$$

Although Q correlations did not provide us with the desired results, perhaps other similarity measures might be profitably used with Q-factor analysis. That question is addressed in the next section where we take a closer look at the many *definitions* of profile similarity.

Measuring Profile Similarity With D^2

In an important article on profile resemblance, Cronbach and Gleser (1953) showed that profile similarity can be defined in severals ways and that the numerical similarity between two profiles can be partitioned into three separately estimable components: elevation, scatter, and shape. In this framework, profile *elevation* equals "the mean of all scores for a given person" (p. 460); profile *scatter* equals "the square root of the sum of squares of the individual's deviation scores about his own mean" (p. 460); and profile *shape* equals "the residual information in the score set after equating profiles for both elevation and scatter" (p. 460). According to these authors, all three of these components are accurately measured by an index called D^2.

Simply put, D^2 equals the sum of squared differences between two profiles. More formally, let j represent the jth variable in a profile of k variables; let i equal the ith profile in a set of N profiles; and let x_{ji} equal the score of person i on variable j. Then, for Subjects 1 and 2,

$$D^2_{12} = \sum_{j=1}^{k} (x_{j1} - x_{j2})^2. \tag{6.3}$$

Although D^2 is one of the few distance measures that is sensitive to all three components of profile resemblance[6] (i.e., elevation, scatter, and shape), the index does have some important limitations. For example, D^2 is also sensitive to the direction of keying of the profile indicators. This means that the relative distance between two profiles can change if one or more variables are scored in the opposite direction. Moreover, D^2 is sensitive to the metric of the variables such that variables with greater

---

[6]Raw sums of squares and cross products also measure these components:

$$SSCP_{12} = \sum_{j=1}^{k} (x_{j1} \times x_{j2})^2.$$

variance can receive more weight than variables with small variance. D^2 is also *not* sensitive to the correlations among the variables.[7]

In this section, we illustrate D^2 and several related measures of profile resemblance with a subset of the person arrays from the dissociation data. Specifically, we use the score profiles from Subjects 1, 2, and 5 of the example data: .

$$
\begin{array}{cccccccccc}
 & D1 & D2 & D3 & D4 & D5 & D6 & D7 & D8 \\
S1 & 80 & 50 & 90 & 65 & 75 & 85 & 100 & 100 \\
S2 & 80 & 15 & 95 & 75 & 100 & 100 & 100 & 80 \\
S5 & 10 & 0 & 0 & 10 & 20 & 0 & 0 & 0
\end{array}.
$$

When these profiles are compared using Equation (6.3), we find that $D^2_{12} = 2,600$, $D^2_{15} = 48,775$, and $D^2_{25} = 51,175$.

In words, the D^2 coefficients indicate that Subjects 1 and 2 are more alike than either Subjects 1 and 5 or Subjects 2 and 5 with respect to the dissociative experiences that are tapped by the DES-T. Likeness in this situation is indexed by the Euclidean distance between the score profiles in the 8-dimensional space that is defined by the DES-T items.

An attractive feature of D^2 is that it simultaneously considers elevation, scatter, and shape when quantifying the similarity between two profiles. In some contexts, however, the investigator may be interested in only one or two of these features of profile similarity. For instance, in the data reported above, the elevations for the first two profiles are large and equal (80.625), whereas the elevation for the fifth profile is considerably smaller (5.00). These differences in elevation influence the relative ordering of the D^2 values. The scatters for the three profiles—which equal 45.52, 75.31, and 20.00—also influence the ordering of the D^2 values. Suppose that in a particular research context we are not interested in these features of resemblance. That is, suppose that we are only interested in comparing profiles with respect to their relative shapes. How do we quantify profile similarity in this situation?

Cronbach and Gleser (1953) demonstrated that D^2 can be easily modified to accommodate various definitions of profile similarity. For example, let D' represent the distance between two profiles that have been centered around their means. A centered profile is one in which the elevation differences have been eliminated.[8] Suppose that Profiles 1 and 2 have been centered. Then it can be shown that

---

[7] A related index called the Mahalanobis distance takes the correlations into account.

[8] This is accomplished by subtracting the profile mean (i.e., the profile elevation) from each profile element.

$$D'^2_{12} = D^2_{12} - k\Delta^2 El_{12} \tag{6.4}$$

where $\Delta^2 El_{12}$ equals the squared *Ele*vation differences (Δ) between Profiles 1 and 2, and k equals the common profile length. In our example, k equals 8; $\Delta^2 El_{12} = 0.00$, and $D\Delta^2 El_{15} = \Delta^2 El_{25} = 5,719.14$. Therefore,

$$D'^2_{12} = 2,600 = 2,600 - 8 \times (80.625 - 80.625)^2 ,$$

$$D'^2_{15} = 3,021.875 = 48,775 - 8 \times (80.625 - 5.00)^2 ,$$

and

$$D'^2_{25} = 5,421.875 = 51,175 - 8 \times (80.625 - 5.00)^2 .$$

In situations where profile shape is important but where elevation and scatter are irrelevant—for example, when profiles have been ipsatized to have means of 0.00 and standard deviations of 1.00—an appropriate distance measure is given by

$$D''^2_{12} = \frac{D'^2_{12} - \Delta^2 S}{S_1 S_2} = \frac{D^2_{12} - k\Delta^2 El_{12} - \Delta^2 S}{S_1 S_2} , \tag{6.5}$$

where S_i is the scatter for profile i, and $\Delta^2 S$ is the squared difference in scatter between the two profiles. For the example data,

$$D''^2_{12} = .50 = \frac{2,600 - (45.518 - 75.312)^2}{45.518 \times 75.312} ,$$

$$D''^2_{15} = 2.604 = \frac{3,021.875 - (45.518 - 20)^2}{45.518 \times 20} ,$$

and

$$D''^2_{25} = 1.568 = \frac{5,421.875 - (75.312 - 20)^2}{75.312 \times 20} .$$

The last index is particularly interesting from the perspective of this chapter because of its relationship to the Q correlation (Q). Specifically, Cronbach and Gleser (1953) have shown that

$$D''^2 = 2(1 - Q), \qquad (6.6)$$

or alternatively,

$$Q = 1 - \frac{D''^2}{2}. \qquad (6.7)$$

These expressions mathematically illustrate why *Q-factor analysis of Q correlations cannot identify taxa that are consistent with the General Covariance Mixture Theorem.*[9] Q correlations, being derivable from D''^2, are not sensitive to profile elevation or scatter differences. This is an important point that can be highlighted by graphically illustrating the three components of profile similarity described by Cronbach and Gleser.

Figure 6.1 shows four possible scalings for the three example profiles. The first panel in the figure displays the subject arrays in their original metric. Notice that in the metric of the raw scores the first two profiles are closer to one another than either is to Profile 5. It is obvious from this plot that elevation is the primary component of profile resemblance in this example. This conclusion is further supported by the next plot, which displays the profiles after elevation has been removed. Notice that by forcing the profiles to have the same means we have concealed the taxonic structure of the data. That is, Profile 5 no longer appears to belong to a separate category because we have redefined the notion of profile similarity. The remaining plots illustrate the consequences of removing scatter differences.

---

[9]Of course, they do not rule out the possibility that Q-factor analysis of Q correlations might be useful in identifying other "types" of taxa, although, quite frankly, we have never seen other types of taxa. Some of our colleagues have suggested that the method identifies subgroups with common correlation structures. Invariably, they concoct a hypothetical example with perhaps 40 individuals and three variables. For 20 individuals, variables 1 and 2 correlate .50, variables 1 and 3 correlate .50, and variables 2 and 3 correlate .45. For the remaining individuals, the respective correlations are the same magnitude but with a negative sign (e.g., variables 1 and 2 correlate −.50). If such samples existed, we would feel comfortable calling them types. We agree that this is an interesting example, *but it is not one that can be accurately analyzed by Q-factor analysis with Q correlations* (we encourage the doubting Thomas to try this example with simulated data).

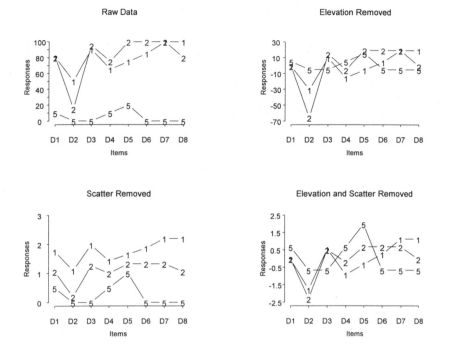

Figure 6.1. Four Possible Scalings of Three Example Profiles

A second means of highlighting the conclusions of this section is to summarize the example data with the four similarity measures described above: Q, D^2, D'^2, and D''^2. We have done this in Table 6.2. As can be seen in this table, D^2 is the only measure that accurately mirrors the taxonic structure of the dissociation data.

Recovering Level Taxa With Q-Factor Analysis

At this point there should be no doubt in your mind that Q-factor analysis with Q correlations cannot recover latent taxa that are consistent with the General Covariance Mixture Theorem. For reasons stated in the previous section, using Q correlations with taxonic data is equivalent to ignoring the information provided by the indicator validities (i.e., the differences

TABLE 6.2 Four Possible Similarity Matrices for the Dissociation Data

				X					Elevation	Scatter
	D1	D2	D3	D4	D5	D6	D7	D8		
S1	80	50	90	65	75	85	100	100	80.625	45.518
S2	80	15	95	75	100	100	100	80	80.625	75.312
S3	85	90	90	70	80	90	85	95	85.625	20.540
S4	10	0	0	0	0	10	10	0	3.750	13.693
S5	10	0	0	10	20	0	0	0	5.000	20.000
S6	0	0	20	0	0	0	15	0	4.375	21.723

Q

$$
\begin{bmatrix}
1.000 & 0.750 & 0.398 & 0.371 & -0.302 & 0.484 \\
 & 1.000 & -0.115 & 0.370 & 0.216 & 0.353 \\
 & & 1.000 & 0.111 & -0.669 & 0.175 \\
 & & & 1.000 & -0.183 & 0.063 \\
 & & & & 1.000 & -0.403 \\
 & & & & & 1.000
\end{bmatrix}
$$

D^2

$$
\begin{bmatrix}
0 & 2600 & 1950 & 49075 & 48775 & 48100 \\
 & 0 & 6650 & 52375 & 51175 & 51500 \\
 & & 0 & 54175 & 53375 & 53550 \\
 & & & 0 & 700 & 625 \\
 & & & & 0 & 1225 \\
 & & & & & 0
\end{bmatrix}
$$

D'^2

$$
\begin{bmatrix}
0 & 2600.000 & 1750.000 & 1796.875 & 3021.875 & 1587.500 \\
 & 0 & 6450.000 & 5096.875 & 5421.875 & 4987.500 \\
 & & 0 & 546.875 & 1371.875 & 737.500 \\
 & & & 0 & 687.500 & 621.875 \\
 & & & & 0 & 1221.875 \\
 & & & & & 0
\end{bmatrix}
$$

D''^2

$$
\begin{bmatrix}
0 & 0.500 & 1.204 & 1.258 & 2.604 & 1.033 \\
 & 0 & 2.230 & 1.261 & 1.568 & 1.293 \\
 & & 0 & 1.778 & 3.339 & 1.650 \\
 & & & 0 & 2.365 & 1.874 \\
 & & & & 0 & 2.806 \\
 & & & & & 0
\end{bmatrix}
$$

in the indicator means between the taxon and complement groups). If Q-factor analysis is to identify level taxa it must be used with similarity measures that are sensitive to profile elevation. We have seen that Cronbach and Gleser's (1953) D^2 coefficient satisfies this criterion. Thus, to complete our comparison of L-Mode and Q-factor analysis, in this section we perform a Q-factor analysis on the D^2 values from the example data. Actually, because D^2 is a *dis*similarity measure—in that larger numbers reflect greater profile differences—we analyze negative D^2 values. Furthermore, to maintain consistency with our previous analyses, the profiles are compared on a variable-standardized matrix.

After scaling the dissociation data so that each item array (column) has a mean of 0.00 and standard deviation of 1.00, the matrix of $-D^2$ values for the six subject arrays (profiles) is given by

$$(-)D^2x_z = \begin{array}{c} \\ S1 \\ S2 \\ S3 \\ S4 \\ S5 \\ S6 \end{array} \begin{array}{cccccc} S1 & S2 & S3 & S4 & S5 & S6 \\ 0 & -1.552 & -1.337 & -24.105 & -23.394 & -23.840 \\ & 0 & -4.599 & -25.750 & -24.508 & -25.521 \\ & & 0 & -28.401 & -27.425 & -28.301 \\ & & & 0 & -0.363 & -0.291 \\ & & & & 0 & -0.613 \\ & & & & & 0 \end{array}.$$

The eigenvectors ($\mathbf{U}^D$) and eigenvalues ($\mathbf{L}^D$) of this matrix equal

$$\mathbf{U}^D = \begin{bmatrix} 0.381 & 0.006 & -0.548 & -0.625 & 0.155 & -0.373 \\ 0.387 & 0.740 & 0.215 & 0.278 & -0.094 & -0.413 \\ 0.438 & -0.671 & 0.271 & 0.280 & -0.049 & -0.452 \\ -0.421 & -0.033 & -0.084 & -0.137 & -0.794 & -0.408 \\ -0.403 & 0.032 & 0.576 & -0.410 & 0.425 & -0.394 \\ -0.417 & -0.010 & -0.491 & 0.516 & 0.393 & -0.406 \end{bmatrix},$$

and

$$Diag(\mathbf{L}^D) = [74.341 \quad 4.583 \quad 0.816 \quad 0.335 \quad 0.214 \quad -80.289].$$

Plugging these values into the formula for a factor structure matrix we get

$$\mathbf{\Lambda}^D = \begin{array}{c} S1 \\ S2 \\ S3 \\ S4 \\ S5 \\ S6 \end{array} \overset{\mathbf{\Lambda}^D}{\begin{bmatrix} 3.286 & 0.013 \\ 3.336 & 1.584 \\ 3.772 & -1.437 \\ -3.631 & -0.070 \\ -3.478 & 0.068 \\ -3.592 & -0.022 \end{bmatrix}} = \overset{\mathbf{U}^D}{\begin{bmatrix} 0.381 & 0.006 \\ 0.387 & 0.740 \\ 0.438 & -0.671 \\ -0.421 & -0.033 \\ -0.403 & 0.032 \\ -0.417 & -0.010 \end{bmatrix}} \cdot \overset{\mathbf{L}^{D\frac{1}{2}}}{\begin{bmatrix} \sqrt{74.341} & 0.000 \\ 0.000 & \sqrt{4.583} \end{bmatrix}}.$$

These results are comforting because they suggest that Q-factor analysis *can* be used with taxonic data. Subjects who dissociate frequently have large positive loadings, and subjects who rarely dissociate have large negative loadings on the first Q-factor. In other words, the individuals with dissociative identity disorder have been correctly distinguished from those who are symptom free. Earlier, we presented an example where L-Mode gave similar results. One difference between these examples is that in the earlier case the group assignments were reflected in the factor scores rather than the factor loadings. This brings up the question of whether the L-Mode factor scores are somehow related to the "Q-Mode" factor loadings. As it turns out, the answer to this question is *yes*. When the Q-factor loadings from the $-D^2$ matrix are standardized to have a mean of 0.00 and standard deviation of 1.00, *the scaled Q-factor loadings* Λ_Z^D *and the L-Mode factor scores are asymptotically equivalent.*[10]

$$\Lambda_Z^D = \begin{matrix} S1 \\ S2 \\ S3 \\ S4 \\ S5 \\ S6 \end{matrix} \begin{bmatrix} .866 \\ .878 \\ .992 \\ -.928 \\ -.889 \\ -.919 \end{bmatrix}.$$

As a final summary, we direct your attention to Figure 6.2, which graphically illustrates the main findings from the three analyses described in this chapter. Notice that of four ways of representing the dissociation data in 2-dimensional space, only the Q-factor loadings of Q correlations fail to elucidate the taxonic structure of the data.

---

[10]In the present example they differ in the third or fourth decimal place because of the loss of a degree of freedom in the item × item correlation matrix for the L-Mode analysis (i.e., $N-1$ was used in the denominators of the correlation coefficients).

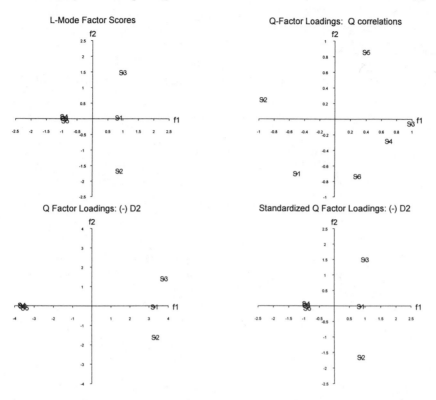

Figure 6.2. A Comparison of L-Mode and Q-Factor Analysis

7 Taxometrics in Scientific Methodology

The glorious endeavor that we know today as science has grown out of the murk of sorcery, religious ritual, and cooking. But while witches, priests, and chefs were developing taller hats, scientists worked out a method for determining the validity of their results: they learned to ask *Are they reproducible?"*

—G. H. Scherr (1983, p. ix)

Imagine that you have a hunch or a theoretically guided suspicion that your favorite construct is taxonic. Further imagine that, being an empiricist, you have collected data on several conjectured taxon indicators and that you have analyzed the data with one of the procedures described in this book. Your analysis reveals that the latent structure of the indicators is taxonic: What do you do now? In this final chapter, we suggest that it is good scientific practice to *always* reanalyze your data with multiple taxometric procedures and to perform multiple consistency tests. Like the opening quote of this chapter, we believe that *replication is the hallmark of science* and that *consistency tests* provide the most scientifically justifiable means of corroborating scientific models.

Guidelines for Corroborating Taxonic Models

Taxometrics is just like any other data analysis procedure in that the mathematics alone does not give us all the answers. It is only a tool for generating numbers that must be interpreted by an embedding text (Meehl, 1990a, 1990b). A mean or a standard deviation is useless unless one knows what the individual scores represent; a correlation coefficient is meaningless without information about what was correlated; a crucial step in factor analysis is naming and interpreting the factors. Likewise, one may find a taxon, but knowing what that taxon represents depends on one's theory and the carefulness with which it is being tested.

Taxometrics is different from most other data analysis procedures in that it looks for—and depends on—coherence within the data rather than merely describing it (as does, say, a mean). We test the data by various (mathematically independent) procedures that provide both consistency tests for one another and multiple epistemic paths to estimating parameters, and in this way we converge upon a knowledge of the true state of affairs. This taxometric approach to analyzing data is motivated by philosophy of science considerations and stems from metatheoretical principles that are not widely understood by social scientists; hence, we discuss some of those principles briefly.

Assessing Scientific Theories

Historians and philosophers of science and a few working scientists with philosophical bent have listed the intrinsic properties and external relations of scientific theories that scientists attend to when appraising theories, devising empirical tests, and amending theories in light of the resulting data. One may ask, for example, whether a theory explains numerous observed facts, or whether it predicts new relationships among observable facts, or how numerically precise are the predictions it makes. No one claims to offer a complete list, and it is worth noting that no two lists are identical; some scholars may lay very strong emphasis on one or another theory property not even included on lists prepared by others. When a particular property is on the list, the question arises what relative importance should be given to it vis-à-vis the other features.

Take, for example, the feature of *novel predictions* in appraising a scientific theory. Some philosophers of science make the strong claim that to be accepted as scientific a theory must generate new predictions; it is not truly scientific if it only explains after the fact the data that suggested it to the theorist's mind. One might assume that holders of this view would take it for granted that successful novel predictions outweigh other features, but that does not directly follow. A metatheorist may consider a theory admissible only if it makes novel predictions, yet hold that within the admissible theories the number or proportion of successful novel predictions as a *quantitative* feature does not countervail ("trump," phi-

losophers often say) all other attributes that competing theories may
possess (e.g., numerical precision, diversity of facts). Historian Brush
(1989, 1995) found from a survey of the writings of eminent Continental,
British, and American physicists during the years immediately following
the famous observation of light bending predicted by Einstein's General
Relativity (GR) that, with only a couple of exceptions, they were not
influenced by this successful novel prediction as much as they were by
GR's success in explaining the aberrant perihelion of Mercury, an anomaly
that had been known for over half a century. Einstein himself wrote to a
friend that when he realized that GR could derive the perihelion anomaly
he went around for two days in a state of ecstasy (Highfield & Carter, 1994,
p. 174). One possible reason for the greater impact on the scientific
community of the perihelion derivation could be that its numerical precision was very high, amounting to an accuracy within one second per
century; whereas the light bending prediction was considerably off (even
after some perhaps tendentious data selection by Eddington [see Earman
& Glymour, 1980]), the observed result deviating from Einstein's prediction by approximately the 10% level of significance (to use the jargon of
social science). Thus, it could be that the numerical precision loomed
larger than novelty when both were not present in the same derivation
chain. We take no stand in this matter, but present this as an example of
metatheoretical disagreement concerning one of the biggest revolutions in
the history of empirical science.

   The only way to appraise the relative importance of theory features is
to combine a priori considerations of logic, semiotics, probability theory,
and epistemology with statistical analysis of archival data on episodes in
the history of science, as proposed by Faust and Meehl (Faust, 1984; Faust
& Meehl, 1992; Meehl, 1983, pp. 371-372, 1992a). In the meantime, we
are forced to rely on armchair reasoning and anecdotal impressions. We
are satisfied that the *riskiness of a prediction* has been given a very heavy
weight in the history of science and properly so. One may use Popperian
terms and speak of risky tests surmounting difficult hurdles; if one does
not subscribe to Popper's orientation but is, say, more a traditional induc-
tivist, one can speak of a Salmonean coincidence.[1] Fortunately, the difference between these two, while of intrinsic interest to philosophers, does

---

[1]Salmon (1984, pp. 213-227) develops the argument that if a theory is false, its ability to
derive a variety of facts (narrowly specified) would be a "strange coincidence." Such an
"explanation" of observational successes the scientist wisely rejects. The more diverse and
narrow are the predictions, the "riskier" the empirical hurdle, according to Popper (1959,
1962, 1983). Cf. Meehl, 1990a, on theory appraisal.

not matter for our purposes because they both lead to the same research strategy and the same preferences in theory appraisal. We are not saying that riskiness is more important than all other features of theories; we only say that it properly gets a high weight in theory appraisal.

Riskiness via Numerically Precise Predictions

One way for a theory to take a risk combines novelty and numerical precision. A scientist whose theory correctly predicts a numerical point value within a very small permitted tolerance in a new experimental context can usually expect that the theory will be appraised extremely favorably, even if other things might speak against it somewhat. There is little, if any, dispute among scientists or philosophers and historians of science that success in deriving narrow-range numerical predictions is properly taken as strong corroboration of a theory. Very strong theories allow us to derive numerical point values or narrow ranges.[2] More commonly, the theory, although not strong enough to perform this striking feat, is able to entail a function form such that with suitable parameter adjustments (they must not be too ad hoc!) one numerical observational value is derivable from one or more others. In the social sciences, theoretically derived point predictions are rare, but one familiar example is that a dominant gene theory of schizotaxia entails that half of the siblings of schizophrenic probands should belong to the taxon.

The concept of numerical precision requires some spelling out. What we mean by it, and what we think the history of science shows it to have meant more often than not, is that the theory tolerates a range of observed values that is small with regard to the antecedent range of numerical possibilities. Following philosopher and statistician von Kries (1886; see Keynes, 1929), we call the antecedent range the *Spielraum* (Meehl, 1990a, 1997). For example, absent any detailed genetic theory, but relying on background knowledge that heredity and environment are relevant to mental disorder, we may ask what is the incidence of the schizotypal taxon (not of clinical schizophrenia) among the siblings of carefully diagnosed schizophrenic probands? It could be anywhere from the 1% lifetime morbidity risk for schizophrenia in the general population to a 100% concordance such as we find for monozygotic twins in more strongly genetic conditions such as

---

[2]For example, James Clerk Maxwell (1831-1879) derived the velocity of light from his electromagnetic field equations.

Huntington's disease. Meehl's dominant gene conjecture (see, e.g., Meehl, 1990d) predicts that the sibling incidence should be 50%, and, with adequate cooperation of the identified families and a sufficiently large sample, we can insist that the observed proportion be within a very few points of the theoretical value $p = 50$. If we got a 30% concordance among the siblings, Meehl's theory would be clearly falsified. If we got a 49% to 53% incidence, the theory would not be proved,[3] but it would have passed a fairly risky test and hence have undergone sizable corroboration.

Taxometrics based on the coherent cut kinetics method was originally devised through reflection on a certain tension among metatheoretical principles as applied to psychopathology. First, one recognizes that only a small proper subset of theoretical terms in empirical science are "operationally defined." The typical introductory psychology or sociology class is more than half a century out of date on this point. The most powerful theoretical concepts in science are not defined operationally nor as some kind of summary of protocols (statistical or otherwise). Rather, they are *implicitly* defined by their role in the postulated theoretical network. This undeniable fact about empirical theories, even in advanced science, leads to the ubiquity of *open concepts* as expounded by Arthur Pap (1953, 1958, chap. 11) in his classic elaboration and amendment of Carnap's (1936-1937) "Testability and Meaning." Theoretical concepts have an unavoidable "openness" for three reasons. First, at all stages in the research enterprise, and strikingly so in the social sciences, the theoretical network is highly incomplete; no theorist claims that all the causal and compositional relations of theoretical concepts are included in the theory as it stands. If

---

[3]Popper, Salmon, and other philosophers of science remind us that data can never *prove* an empirical theory; it can only corroborate the theory. For instance, Newton's theory of gravitation implies that material bodies mutually attract one another. Over the years, scientists found corroborating evidence for the theory in numerous and diverse phenomena, such as the behavior of falling bodies, the motions of the tides, and the orbits of the planets. Enough evidence had accumulated by the turn of this century that many scientists believed that Newton's theory was proved. In his theory of relativity, Einstein later showed that Newton's laws are not universally valid. Most of what Kuhn (1962) calls "normal science" is not aimed at theory appraisal—the theory is taken for granted as being substantially correct—but at explaining apparent discrepancies, improving numerical estimates, trying new applications, relating the theory to theories "above" or "below" it in the pyramid of sciences (*reduction*), amendment of auxiliary theories, and the like (see, e.g., Mayo, 1996, for a discussion of this). In the future of taxometrics, the various consistency tests will be differentially employed to examine different portions of the theoretical network (e.g., appraising the accuracy of different latent value estimates) once it is assumed that the structural conjecture of taxonicity has been corroborated. See Salmon (1973) for an edifying and entertaining discussion of the role of data in theory confirmation.

our theories were complete, why would scientists be doing research? Second, the links or connections (causal or compositional) among theoretical entities are usually not strict (i.e., nomological), but are stochastic (probabilistic). Third, the *nature* of the theoretical entities remains to be ascertained (e.g., a gene is a cistron is a sequence of codons). All theories in the social sciences are "open" in these three senses (cf. Meehl, 1972, p. 21, 1977, 1986, 1990c; Meehl & Golden, 1982, pp. 136-138).

How can open concepts defined implicitly by a loose net of connections be susceptible to strong, "risky" numerical tests? How can we admit or even insist on the intrinsic conceptual looseness or fuzziness of theoretical concepts—especially in the primitive stages of a science and permanently in sciences like psychology or sociology which will remain largely stochastic in their lawlike statements—and yet require numerical precision and novelty capable of generating risky tests of those theories? Once one sees clearly what the problem is, the formulation is fairly obvious: We *must statisticize the openness.* This means not merely the familiar, unavoidable use of statistical formulas to take account of sampling and measurement error in quantifying the observables. It means that the formalism associated with theoretical discourse attaches probability numbers to the inferred states, properties, frequencies, conditional probabilities, correlations, and so forth of the theoretical entities themselves. This intrinsically stochastic inbuilt feature of theory would exist if there were no measurement errors or sampling problems. The inferred entities are probabilified, as they are in fields such as genetics, quantum mechanics, epidemiology, and the kinetic theory of heat.

Numerical Predictions in Taxometrics

Only a few scientific theories are capable of generating numerical predictions from qualitative postulates, even when the latter are combined with conjectured function forms (e.g., parabola, growth function), because the laws typically involve numerical parameters that are not derivable from the qualitative conceptualization. Such cases overwhelmingly preponderate in the social sciences (behavior genetics, relying on the background knowledge about the statistics of genes, is a rare exception). Instead, the riskiness has to come from intradata inference, that is, from using the numerical values in suitably chosen proper subsets of the data to infer numerical values of other subsets of the data with a sufficiently narrow tolerance to constitute a high risk. The inference cannot rely solely on the general transformation rules of mathematics and logic, of course, but must depend on those postulates of the formalism as motivated and interpreted by the associated theoretical text that make one theory significantly different from its competitors.

Distinguishing between the *designatum* (meaning, concept, definition) of a theoretical term and its *denotatum* (referent, realized external object), one reasons that if a certain derivation chain involving some combination of interpretive text and formalism includes a theoretical expression that does not denote (and assuming, of course, that the terminus of the derivation chain is a theorem not of general mathematics but requires some theoretical postulates as well), there is no reason to expect that observational numbers, when plugged into the derived theorem, will satisfy it. Note we cannot say that it *must* be false. This would be the formal fallacy of denying the antecedent, as bad as the fallacy of affirming the consequent.[4] All we can say is that if the observational tolerance is small in relationship to the *Spielraum*, then, since there is no theoretical reason for expecting the theorem to be true, if the theory is false we would have a Salmonean coincidence—in other words, the theory would have passed a risky test.

In the broadest sense, a consistency test is an algorithmic procedure that operates on observed or inferred quantities to yield a derived numerical value that should, within tolerance, agree with a numerical value derived differently and not shown to be equal by virtue of a mathematical identity. We emphasize that taxometric analysis is not unique in this respect. The use of the phrase "consistency test" as a term of art in taxometrics can mislead one to think that this is some special sort of empirical scientific

---

[4]Affirming the consequent and denying the antecedent are two types of fallacious reasoning.

Here is an example that illustrates the illogic of **Affirming the Consequent**:

If: Meehl's theory of schizophrenia is correct, half of the siblings of schizophrenic probands should be schizotaxic.

And: Half of the siblings of schizophrenic probands are schizotaxic.

Then: Meehl's theory is correct.

This example illustrates the illogic of **Denying the Antecedent**:

If: Meehl's theory of schizophrenia is correct, half of the siblings of schizophrenic probands should be schizotaxic.

And: Meehl's theory is incorrect.

Then: Not half of the siblings of schizophrenic probands are schizotaxic.

Empirically speaking, in both of these examples the conclusion reached is not certain because half of the siblings could be schizotaxic due to some other theoretical state of affairs. Both syllogisms are *formally* invalid when treated as logical deductions.

procedure peculiar to, if not taxometrics, at least psychometrics or social science—but that is wrong. Looking for the convergence of numerical values reached by different empirical paths is so much taken for granted in the developed sciences like astronomy, physics, chemistry, geology, and genetics that scientists in those fields have not found it necessary to give this approach a special methodological name.

It is possible for a constant or variable in the formalism of an empirical science to denote even though the corresponding term in the interpretive text is nondenoting. For example, in taxometrics, the symbol P designates a base rate; on that interpretation, if there is no taxon, if the latent structure is that of, say, a unimodal single factor rather than two overlapping distributions, if P is supposed to stand for the base rate of a taxon and there isn't any taxon, we might say that P does not denote. But while the phrase "base rate" (taken to be quantified by the number P inferred from our statistics) may not denote if the latent structure is nontaxonic and we are erroneously treating it as if it were, it is possible that the *number P* inferred from our manifest statistics does denote, but in that nontaxonic case it denotes something other than the base rate of a taxon. An obvious candidate under some circumstances would be that P denotes the integral of some underlying factor's density function from a certain cutting score up,

$$P = \int_{x_c}^{\infty} \Phi(x) \mathrm{d}x.$$

Since the history of science presents us with instances in which false theories have survived risky tests, the notion of surmounting a risky hurdle or achieving a Salmonean strange coincidence must be carefully stated as a guideline, a rule of thumb, as something speaking in a theory's favor, rather than as a *rule*. It cannot be taken as a litmus test of the theory having truth or extremely high verisimilitude (cf. Carrier, 1991; Meehl, 1992c).

The two big taxometric questions presented by a data set are (a) the threshold question "Is the latent structure taxonic or not?" and (b) "What is the relative frequency P of taxon members?" Given trustworthy answers to these two questions, investigators will differ in their concern with how accurate other inferences are. For example, a researcher testing a dominant gene theory of schizotaxia needs to know the taxon rate among siblings of schizophrenic probands very accurately, but the valid and false positive rates of the several indicators at the hitmax cut may be of little interest. A clinician concerned with optimum treatment choices would have a strong interest in these latter values and might not care much about the precision of the base-rate estimate. For this reason, the ideal knowledge situation as to consistency tests would be a battery of them chosen for differential sensitivity to different inferential errors. For example, a multivariate equation yielding expected algebraic error Δh_b (in hit rate below the hitmax cut) and expected absolute error $|\Delta h_b|$ as a function of consistency tests $C_1, C_2 \ldots C_k$ would permit investigators to set up their own tolerances on the basis of their own research programs and clinical tasks. There should be a set of such equations for the taxonic/nontaxonic dichotomy and for the expected algebraic and absolute errors in estimating such parameters as base rate, hitmax cut location, valid and false positive and negative rates and total hit rate yielded by that cut, proportion of all cases above and below the hitmax cut, latent taxon and complement means and standard deviations and indicator latent separations, and diagnostic probabilities for individuals sorted by Bayes's Rule. Developing such an equation system will be a major research task. In the meantime, one may use a rough classification of samples as "passing" or "failing" successive hurdles in a consistency test set, the hurdle cuts being based on allowed tolerances of error in inferring the important latent parameters, as was done by Meehl and Golden (1982).

Convergence among partially or wholly independent estimates of a conjectural latent numerical value is corroborative, but it cannot be viewed as a clincher argument. When the intepretive text associated with the taxometric formalism contains a nondenoting theoretical term it is tempting to infer directly that the formalism element itself is therefore nondenoting; and, hence, if a numerical value assigned to it comes out right, in the sense of correctly predicting some other numerical value or getting the same numerical value by different indicators or different mathematical derivation chains, this constitutes a highly unlikely coincidence. It is in many cases unlikely but not always, and one cannot be confident without further investigation whether the instant case is among the unlikely ones. As stated previously, the reason why immediate inference from nondenoting theoretical text to a nondenoting parameter, variable, or function in the formalism is unsound is that a parameter or variable may have a numerical value corresponding to *some* theoretical entity but not the one designated by the text. For example, one might mistakenly infer latent taxonicity from a marginal MAXCOV graph and find that the inferred base rate is estimated to be .50. Using nonoverlapping sets of indicators or using the same set of indicators with a different procedure (e.g., MAMBAC; see Meehl & Yonce, 1994) will yield consistent values because the algebra that estimates the base rate for a taxonic situation yields a value of about .50 for a nontaxonic situation. As we mentioned previously, we might properly say that this pseudo-"base rate" probably denotes some quantitative feature of the latent distribution (e.g., the integral of a latent factor distribution from the median up); but, although that "base rate" value stands for something that is physically there, it cannot be the base rate of a taxon because there isn't any taxon.

The possibility of this happening warns us that while *inconsistency* of base-rate estimates may be quite satisfactory as an indicator of nontaxonicity or suggestive of some gross metric or sampling error problem within a taxonic structure, their *consistency* cannot be relied on as assurance against a pseudotaxon. Therefore, one would need to supplement coherency of base-rate estimates by other consistency tests described here and in other publications by the authors. It will probably be desirable ultimately to distinguish between consistency tests that are mainly sensitive to errors in the model (i.e., pseudotaxonicity) and others which, working within an objectively correct taxonic model, are responsive to biases or extreme sampling fluctuations such that some of the inferred latent values are likely to be untrustworthy.

The problem takes a special form in taxometrics or in other kinds of psychometric analysis of data patterns, but it exemplifies a more general problem in scientific metatheory concerning the danger of making strong inferences from Salmonean coincidences. Case studies in the history of science present us with surprising—sometimes shocking—examples of highly successful numerical derivations which were fruitful in producing scientific progress, and which turned out nevertheless to be not only numerically incorrect at a theoretical level but even qualitatively erroneous. For example, Niels Bohr received a Nobel prize for his brilliant derivation of the hydrogen spectrum and a quite precise derivation of the Rydberg constant, both derived from his quantization of the Rutherford atomic model (Pais, 1991). The theoretical quantity *mvr* plays a central role in Bohr's derivation chain, being the quantification of the energy level of the rotating electron in the stationary state, that is, between "quantum jumps." But *mvr*, the angular momentum of a revolving body, is a concept from classical mechanics; modern quantum theory says that no such motion takes place in a stationary state. Thus, he got the right observational answer, including prediction of novel findings in the extended spectrum of hydrogen, by evoking a process that does not even occur. For another example, in the controversy as to whether light impinging on a surface has an impact momentum (the "light pressure" problem), a classic experiment treated for many years as definitive got the right numerical answer "accidentally" by combining four errors (one in the mathematics, three in experimental constants). These errors were just right to cancel out and so erroneously derive a numerical result within 1% of what Maxwell had predicted. For 30 years, physicists relied on this pseudocorroboration of a theory (which is, nevertheless, correct) (Worrall, 1982). The phlogiston theory and caloric theory both made successful novel predictions, but each of them lacks substantive truth (Carrier, 1991; Meehl, 1992c). Given these concerns, the development of numerous independent consistency tests and the analytical or Monte Carlo determination of how much weight each should have and which features of the model it is sensitive to have a high priority in taxometric research.

Corroborating taxonic models is a serious undertaking that requires sophisticated taxometric procedures. In this book we have described several techniques that have proved valuable in our own taxometric research. The source code for these procedures is provided in the appendices that follow. We hope these programs make it easier for you to divide data "according to the natural formation, where the joint is not breaking any part as a bad carver might" (Plato, as cited in the *Phaedrus*). In other words, we hope our taxometric routines help you *carve nature at its joints*.

Appendix A
The Effect of Nuisance Covariance
on L-Mode Parameter Estimates

In many taxometric situations, the assumption of zero nuisance covariance is untenable (Meehl, 1995b). Fortunately, the Monte Carlo results reported in Chapter 5 suggest that L-Mode parameter estimates are not seriously degraded by moderate departures from this assumption. Nevertheless, larger departures may hamper our ability to accurately estimate key taxonic parameters, and it is important therefore to consider the precise means by which nuisance covariance biases L-Mode parameter estimates. Here we consider the effects of nuisance covariance on L-Mode factor loadings.

We first consider a taxometric procedure, recently introduced by Golden (1991), that allows nuisance covariance to arise from a common, *dimensional* factor in the taxon and complement groups. Golden's model can be expressed as follows:

$$z_t = \alpha + \lambda \xi_t + \psi \eta_t + D, \qquad (A.1)$$

$$z_c = \alpha + \lambda \xi_c + \psi \eta_c, \qquad (A.2)$$

where

z_t and z_c are vectors of manifest scores (for a single variate) in the
taxon and complement classes

α is the equation intercept term

ξ represents the vector of common, real-valued factor scores

η represents the vector of real-valued unique (residual) factor scores

λ and ψ are the common and unique factor loadings (regression
weights) for a single variate

D is a conjectured causal factor that shifts the taxon indicator
distribution by an additive constant

Golden suggested that the above equations might apply when D represents
the causal effects of a single major gene and ξ (the common factor scores)
represents disease liability due to multifactorial inheritance.

Starting from a similar position, we have developed a related model for
representing nuisance covariance in a factor-analytic context. In our
model, the conjectured causal factor, D, shifts the liability distribution ξ
in the taxon class, and the resulting shift on z is proportional to the manifest
indicator's factor loading (λ). For the general case,

$$z_t = \alpha + \lambda_t(\xi_t + D) + \psi_t\eta_t,\qquad\text{(A.3)}$$

and

$$z_c = \alpha + \lambda_c(\xi_c) + \psi_c\eta_c,\qquad\text{(A.4)}$$

One advantage of our model is that the influence of D is now placed in the
metric of the (common) factor scores. Moreover, and without loss of
generality, we can assume that D is the expected value of the shifted taxon
distribution (of factor scores) such that $E[\xi_t + D] = D$ and $E[\xi_c] = 0$. Note
that as currently formalized, we have *not* assumed that the regression
weights (i.e., factor loadings) are equal across taxonomic classes. Our
modification of Golden's model provides insight into the effects of nuisance covariance on L-Mode parameter estimates.

Let the subscript **m** represent parameters in a mixed sample of taxon and
complement members. The question that concerns us is the following: *If
the common factor model holds in the taxon and complement classes, what*

is the influence of the conjectured causal factor on the factor pattern in the mixed sample? The following identities and equations, which consider the parameters of the factor analysis model from a taxometric perspective, will help us answer this important question. Let

$$C_t = cov(z_t, \xi_t + D) \tag{A.5}$$

denote the covariance between indicator z and the dimensional factor scores in the taxon class. Let

$$C_c = cov(z_c, \xi_c) \tag{A.6}$$

denote the covariance between indicator z and the dimensional factor scores in the complement class. Let

$$\Phi_t = var(\xi_t + D) \tag{A.7}$$

denote the variance of the factor scores in the taxon class. Let

$$\Phi_c = var(\xi_c) \tag{A.8}$$

denote the variance of the factor scores in the complement class. Then, the regression weight (unstandardized factor loading) that is obtained when the indicator scores (z_t) are regressed on the common factor scores (ξ_t) in the taxon class equals

$$\lambda_t = C_t \Phi_t^{-1}. \tag{A.9}$$

This implies that Equation (A.5), which denotes the covariance between $\mathbf{z}_t$ and ξ_t, can also be expressed as

$$C_t = cov(z_t, \xi_t + D) = \lambda_t \Phi_t. \tag{A.10}$$

Following similar logic, the regression weight (unstandardized factor loading) of z_c and ξ_c (the factor scores in the complement class) is given by

$$\lambda_c = C_c \Phi_c^{-1}, \tag{A.11}$$

and the corresponding covariance term equals

$$C_c = cov(z_c, \xi_c) = \lambda_c \Phi_c. \qquad (A.12)$$

Let

$$E[\xi_t + D] = D \qquad (A.13)$$

denote the expected value of the factor scores in the taxon class, and let

$$E[\xi_c] = 0 \qquad (A.14)$$

denote the expected value of the factor scores in the complement class. Following standard factor-analytic assumptions, we also let

$$E[\eta_t] = E[\eta_c] = 0 \qquad (A.15)$$

denote the expected values of the unique factor scores in the taxon and complement classes.

The above definitions imply that

$$E[z_t] = \alpha + \lambda_t D, \qquad (A.16)$$

and

$$E[z_c] = \alpha \qquad (A.17)$$

which further implies that the expected value of z in the mixed sample equals

$$E[z_m] = P(\alpha + \lambda_t D) + Q(\alpha). \qquad (A.18)$$

Moreover, from the General Covariance Mixture Theorem, the expected covariance between z_m and ξ_m is given by

$$\begin{aligned} C_m &= P\lambda_t \Phi_t + Q\lambda_c \Phi_c + PQ(E[z_t] - E[z_c])(D - 0) \\ &= P\lambda_t \Phi_t + Q\lambda_c \Phi_c + PQ\lambda_t D^2. \end{aligned} \qquad (A.19)$$

To derive the expected factor loading in the mixed sample, we need expressions for the variances of the indicator and common factor scores. Relying on previously defined extensions of the General Covariance Mixture Theorem (Equation [3.3]) we find that

$$var(z_m) = P(\lambda_t \Phi_t \lambda_t + \psi_t^2) + Q(\lambda_c \Phi_c \lambda_c + \psi_c^2) + PQ\lambda_t^2 D^2, \quad (A.20)$$

where ψ_t^2 and ψ_c^2 equal the variances of the uniqueness scores in the taxon and complement classes and

$$var(\xi_m) = P\Phi_t + Q\Phi_c + PQD^2. \tag{A.21}$$

Therefore, the *standardized* factor loading in the mixed sample (which is the result we are after) is as follows:

$$\lambda_m = \frac{P\lambda_t \Phi_t + Q\lambda_c \Phi_c + PQ\lambda_t D^2}{\sqrt{P(\lambda_t \Phi_t \lambda_t + \psi_t^2) + Q(\lambda_c \Phi_c \lambda_c + \psi_c^2) + PQ\lambda_t^2 D^2}} \cdot \frac{(A.22)}{\sqrt{P\Phi_t + Q\Phi_c + PQD^2}}.$$

An important implication of these equations is that L-Mode yields biased estimates of the taxon and complement mean profiles in data matrices with appreciable within-class indicator covariation. Methods to reduce this bias have yet to be developed.

* * *

The following appendixes contain example programs for a suite of taxometric procedures and utility functions. All programs were written in *S*-Plus (StatSci, 1993), a computer language with superb graphics and a wealth of high-level statistical and mathematical routines. *S*-Plus offers an interactive programming environment and researchers should have little difficulty modifying our functions to suit their specific needs.

Readers are encouraged to try these programs on their own data sets. Although the programs have been carefully tested, neither we nor the publisher accept any liabilities regarding their use. Specific questions concerning program code can be addressed to the first author via his e-mail address: ngwaller@ucdavis.edu

All analyses reported in this book were conducted with *S*-Plus version 3.3 for Windows.

Appendix B

This appendix presents source code for three programs: **MAXCOV**, a program for estimating MAXCOV-HITMAX parameters (Meehl, 1973; Meehl & Golden, 1982); **SCORMAX**, a program for estimating Bayesian taxon membership probabilities; and **COMB**, a program for determining all possible MAXCOV indicator combinations. Updated versions of these programs and additional taxometric software can be downloaded from Niels Waller's web page.

http://psychology.ucdavis.edu/waller/default.html

MAXCOV

DESCRIPTION

Returns a MAXCOV-HITMAX plot, a latent class distribution plot, and various taxometric parameter estimates

USAGE

```
MAXCOV(x, y, z, slabsize = 0.25, metric =
"continuous", title = "Maxcov-Hitmax Plot",
minslabsize = 10, smu = "smu.loess")
```

REQUIRED ARGUMENTS

x, y, z score vectors for three conjectured taxon indicators.

OPTIONAL ARGUMENTS

- **slabsize**: the xslab (sorted indicator variable) interval width; for continuous data, **slabsize** is in standard deviation units; for example, **slabsize = .25** instructs the program to construct slabsizes of 1/4 σ width
- **metric**: a character string specifying whether indicators y and z are "continuous" or "binary"
- **title**: a title (enclosed in quotes) for the MAXCOV plot
- **minslabsize**: the minimum number of cases allowed in an xslab
- **smu**: a character string specifying whether the conditional covariances are to be smoothed; optional values include: "**smu.loess**" for a localized regression smoother, "**smu.tukey**" for a running medians smoother due to Tukey (4(3RSR)2H *twice*), and "**none**" for no smoothing

If the program runs to completion, it produces the following output:

- A MAXCOV-HITMAX plot of the observed and possibly smoothed conditional y, z covariances
- A plot of the latent taxonomic class distributions on indicator x
- $\hat{P}$: the estimated taxon base rate
- $\hat{Q}$: the estimated complement base rate
- $\hat{K}$: the estimated crude latent validity for standardized indicators y and z; in other words,

$$(\hat{\bar{y}}_t - \hat{\bar{y}}_c)(\hat{\bar{z}}_t - \hat{\bar{z}}_c)$$

- A returned matrix that includes the lower and upper boundaries of the xslabs; the xslab conditional (y, z) covariances; the xslab conditional probability of taxon membership, P.x; and the xslab conditional number of taxon and complement members, Nt.x and Nc.x, respectively.

MAXCOV Program Code

```
MAXCOV <- function (x, y, z, slabsize = 0.25, metric = "continuous", title = "Maxcov-
Hitmax Plot", minslabsize = 4, smu = "none")
{
#=================================================================#
# S-Plus code for: MAXCOV-HITMAX                                  #
#=================================================================#
xyz <- data.frame(x, y, z)
xyzraw <- xyz


if(metric=="continuous")
    {
    xyz<-apply(xyz, 2, scale)                    #standardize data#
    cutx<-seq(min(x), max(x), slabsize)      #cutx = xslab boundaries#
    }
    else if(metric == "binary")
    {
    slabsize <- 1
    cutx <- seq(-1, max(xyz[, 1]), slabsize)
    }
xyz <- xyz[sort.list(xyz[, 1]), ]     #sort y and z on indicator x#
#-------------------------initialize covvec & Nvec ------------------#
    covvec <- vector("numeric", length(cutx) - 1)    #covvec holds cov(y,z)|x#
    Nvec <- vector("numeric", length(cutx) - 1)      #Nvec holds N in xslab#
#-------------------------------------------------------------------#
#create data slabs
#subxyz = subset of data within xslab,                              #
#-------------------------------------------------------------------#
    for(i in 1:(length(cutx)-1)) {
```

```
        subxyz <- xyz[(xyz[, 1]> cutx[i] & xyz[, 1] <= cutx[i + 1]), ]#
#----------------------------------------------------------------------#
# check dimensions of subxyz and record N subj in interval             #
#----------------------------------------------------------------------#
        if(is.null(dim(subxyz)))
        {
                covvec[i] <- NA
                Nvec[i] <- 0
                next
        }
        else
        {
                Nvec[i] <- length(subxyz[, 1])
        }
        if(subxyz[1] != "NA")
        {
#----------------------------------------------------------------------#
#if N >= minslabsize: compute conditional covariances                  #
#----------------------------------------------------------------------#
        if(length(subxyz[, 1]) < minslabsize)
                {
                print(cat(cutx[i + 1], "N too small!", "\n"))
                covvec[i] <- NA
                next
                }
        if(is.null(dim(subxyz)))
                {
                print(cat(cutx[i + 1], covvec[i], "dim=0", "\n"))
                covvec[i] <- NA
                next
                }
```

```
          covmat <- var(subxyz[, 2:3])
              if(covmat[1] == 0)
          {
              covvec[i] <- 0
          }
                  else
          {
              covvec[i] <- covmat[1, 2]
          }
      }
      else
      {
          covvec[i]<- NA
      }
      print(cat(round(cutx[i + 1], 3), " ", round(covvec[i], 3), " ", Nvec[i], "\n"))
  }
#
#----------------------------------------------------------------------#
# Plot MAXCOV-HITMAX function                                          #
#----------------------------------------------------------------------#
#calculate max and min values for y-axis of MAXCOV plot#
ystats <- summary(covvec)
ymin <- ystats[1] - 0.1
ymax <- ystats[6] + 0.2
xmax <- max(xyz[, 1]) + 0.1
xmin <- -4
if(xmax <= 4)
xmax <- 4
xval <- cutx[2:length(cutx)] # set plotting parameters#
    win.graph()
    par(cex = 0.85, font = 1, lab = c(18, 5, 5))
    plot((xval-(0.5 * slabsize)), covvec, main = title, xlab =
```

112

```r
            "X-slabs", ylab = "Cov(y, z)|x", xlim = c(xmin, xmax), ylim
            = c(ymin, ymax))                                 #
#plot MAXCOV function with possible running medians or loess smoother#
        smoothcov <- na.omit(data.frame(xval-(0.5 * slabsize), covvec))  #
        if(smu == "smu.tukey")
        {
            smoothcov[, 2] <- smooth(smoothcov[, 2])
        }
        else if(smu == "smu.loess")
        {
            smoothcov[, 2] <- loess(smoothcov[,2]~ smoothcov[, 1], span
                = 1)$fitted.values
        }
        lines(x = smoothcov[, 1], y = smoothcov[, 2])#
#-------find maximum of smoothed covariances-------#
        maxcovindex <- (1:length(smoothcov[, 2]))[smoothcov[, 2] == max(
            smoothcov[, 2])]        #
        if(maxcovindex == length(smoothcov[, 2]) | maxcovindex == 1)
        {
            print(cat("\n", "Hitmax at boundary", "\n"))
            stop()
        }

#-------Find hitmax cut from smoothed MAXCOV function-------#
        hitmax <- smoothcov[maxcovindex, 1]        #
#-------calculate crude latent validity K-------#
        K <- 4 * smoothcov[maxcovindex, 2]        #
#-------solve quadratic for p in xslab-------#
        numerator <- sqrt(K^2 - (4 * K * smoothcov[, 2]))
        p1 <- (K - numerator)/(2 * K)
        p2 <- (K + numerator)/(2 * K)
        pxslab <- c(p1[1:maxcovindex], p2[(maxcovindex + 1):length(p2)])  #
```

113

```
#------any probabilities out of bounds?------#
    pxslab[pxslab < 0] <- 0
    pxslab[pxslab > 1] <- 1            #
    qxslab <- 1 - pxslab              #
#------calculate number of taxon and nontaxon members in xslab------#
    Ntxslab <- Nvec[Nvec >= minslabsize] * pxslab      #
    Ncxslab <- Nvec[Nvec >= minslabsize] * qxslab      #
#------plot latent taxonomic class distributions------#
    win.graph()         #
#------midpoints of xslabs------#
    xval <- xval[Nvec >= minslabsize]-(0.5 * slabsize)
    matplot(xval, cbind(Ntxslab, Ncxslab), xlim = c(-4, 4), main =
        "Latent Taxonomic Class Distributions",xlab = "Indicator",
        ylab = "Frequency", type = "l")   #
#------calculate base rate------#
    base.rate <- sum(Ntxslab)/(sum(Ntxslab) + sum(Ncxslab))   #
    px.t <- (0.5 * (Ntxslab[maxcovindex] + sum(Ntxslab[(maxcovindex + 1):
        length(Ntxslab)]))/sum(Ntxslab)
    px.c <- (0.5 * (Ncxslab[maxcovindex] + sum(Ncxslab[(maxcovindex + 1):
        length(Ncxslab)]))/sum(Ncxslab)   #
#------print results------#
    print(cat("\n\n", "Smoothing function = ", smu, "\n"))
    print(cat("\n", "Hitmax (for standardized indicator) = ", round(
        hitmax, 3), "\n"))
    print(cat(" P = ", round(base.rate, 3), "\n"))
    print(cat(" Q = ", round(1-base.rate, 3), "\n"))
    print(cat(" Crude latent validity (for standardized y & z), K =",
        round(K, 3), "\n"))
    covvec <- round(covvec[Nvec >= minslabsize], 3)#
    lowlimit <- round(xval-(0.5 * slabsize), 3)
    lowlimit <- paste(as.character(lowlimit), "+",sep = "")
```

```
   lowlimit <- paste(lowlimit, "thru",sep = " ")
   uplimit <- round(xval + (0.5 * slabsize), 3)
   results <- data.frame(lowlimit, uplimit, covvec, round(pxslab, 3),
         round(Ntxslab, 3), round(Ncxslab, 3))
   names(results) <- c("x.low ", "x.high", "Cov(y,z)|x", "P.x", "Nt.x", "Nc.x")   #
#--------calculate indicator validity---------#
   print(cat(" px.t for dichotomized x =",round(px.t, 3), "\n"))
   print(cat(" px.c for dichotomized x =",round(px.c, 3), "\n\n\n"))
   return(results)
   }
```

SCORMAX

DESCRIPTION

Calculates Bayesian taxon membership probabilities and taxometric consistency tests using output from MAXCOV.

USAGE

```
SCORMAX(data.matrix, hitvec, P.est, px.t.vec, px.c.vec)
```

REQUIRED ARGUMENTS

- **data.matrix**: a matrix of indicator scores
- **hitvec**: a vector of estimated hitmax thresholds from MAXCOV
- **P.est**: the average (or median) base rate from MAXCOV
- **px.t.vec**: a vector of estimated prob(x|t) from MAXCOV
- **px.c.vec**: a vector of estimated prob(x|c) from MAXCOV

If the program runs to completion, it produces the following output:

- Bayesian estimated taxon membership probabilities
- Histogram of the estimated taxon membership probabilities
- Smoothed densities of the latent taxonomic class distributions
- Estimated latent validity cross-products matrix (K)
- Estimated within-class indicator means: $\hat{\mu}_t$ and $\hat{\mu}_c$
- Estimated within-class indicator variances: $\hat{\sigma}_t^2$ and $\hat{\sigma}_c^2$
- Estimated indicator correlation matrices for taxon and nontaxon members
- Observed indicator correlation matrix
- Predicted indicator correlation matrix
- Residual (observed – predicted) indicator correlation matrix
- Goodness of Fit index (GFI) for taxonic model

SCORMAX Program Code

```
SCORMAX <- function (data.matrix, hitvec, P.est, px.t.vec, px.c.vec)
{
#=================================================================#
#SCORMAX                                                          #
#=================================================================#
#--------------standardize data matrix---------------------------#
data.raw <- data.matrix # save backup copy of data#
data.sum <- apply(data.matrix, 1, sum)
data.matrix <- apply(data.matrix, 2, scale)
Q.est <- 1-P.est            #initial estimate of Q: 1- base rate#
nitems <- ncol(data.matrix)
nsubjs <- nrow(data.matrix) #
px.t.vec<-matrix(px.t.vec,nrow=nsubjs,ncol=nitems,byrow=T)
px.c.vec<-matrix(px.c.vec,nrow=nsubjs,ncol=nitems,byrow=T)
qx.t.vec <- 1-px.t.vec #prob of taxon member _not_ endorsing x#
qx.c.vec <- 1-px.c.vec #prob of nontaxon member _not_ endorsing x#
#
#--------------------initialize matrix for binary scores---------#
binary <- matrix(0, nrow = nsubjs, ncol = nitems) #
#
#------cut continuous indicators at hitmax threshold-------------#
for(i in 1:nitems)
     {
     binary[data.matrix[, i] >= hitvec[i], i] <- 1
     }
#
#------calculate probability of x given taxon member------------#
px.tilda.t <- apply((px.t.vec^binary * qx.t.vec^(1-binary)), 1, prod)
px.tilda.c <- apply((px.c.vec^binary * qx.c.vec^(1-binary)), 1, prod) #

#calculate (Bayesian) probability of taxon membership given x#
```

```
pt.x.tilda <- (P.est * px.tilda.t)/(P.est * px.tilda.t + Q.est * px.tilda.c)
win.graph()
hist(pt.x.tilda, breaks = seq(0, 1, 0.1), xlab =
    "Pr(taxon membership)", ylab = "N", main =
    "Bayesian Taxon membership Probabilities")          #
#------plot latent class distributions for total scores------#
dataz <- scale(data.sum)   #

#------assign subjects to latent classes------#
data.c <- dataz[pt.x.tilda < 0.5]
data.t <- dataz[pt.x.tilda > 0.5]   #

#------compute densities for each latent class------#
datac.den <- density(data.c)
datat.den <- density(data.t)   #

#------plot smoothed densities for each latent class------#
win.graph()
plot(smooth(datac.den$x), smooth(datac.den$y), xlim =
    c(-4, 4), xlab = "", ylab = "", ylim = c(0, 2), type = "l")
par(new = T)
plot(smooth(datat.den$x), smooth(datat.den$y), xlim = c(-4, 4), xlab = "Total score",
    ylab = "Density of total score", ylim = c(0, 2), type = "l", main =
    "Latent Taxonomic Class Distributions")   #

#----compute within class inidcator means and crude latent validities----#
mu.t <- apply(data.matrix[pt.x.tilda > 0.5, ], 2, mean)
mu.c <- apply(data.matrix[pt.x.tilda < 0.5, ], 2, mean)
validity <- mu.t - mu.c   #

#----latent validity cross products matrix----#
K.matrix <- as.matrix(validity) %*% t(as.matrix(validity))
obs.cov <- var(data.matrix)   #
```

118

```
#---------within class variances---------#
var.t <- apply(data.matrix[pt.x.tilda > 0.5, ], 2, var)
var.c <- apply(data.matrix[pt.x.tilda < 0.5, ], 2, var)
pred.v.temp <- P.est * var.t + Q.est * var.c #

#---------predicted total correlation matrix---------#
predict.cov <- (K.matrix * P.est * Q.est) + diag(pred.v.temp) #
#---------average off-diagonal correlation---------#
avg.offdiag <- function(x)
{
    return(sum(x-diag(diag(x)))/(nrow(x)^2 - nrow(x)))
}
#
print(avg.offdiag(predict.cov))
#---------within class correlation matrices---------#
cor.t <- cor(data.matrix[pt.x.tilda > 0.5, ])
cor.c <- cor(data.matrix[pt.x.tilda < 0.5, ]) #

#---------print results---------#
print(cat("          Consistency Tests", "\n"))
print(cat("Latent validity cross products matrix (K)", "\n"), quote = F)
print(round(K.matrix, 3))
print(cat("\n\n"))
print(cat("Within class Indicator Means", "\n"), quote = F)
print(round(rbind(mu.t, mu.c), 3))
print(cat("\n\n"))
print(cat("Within class Indicator Variances", "\n"), quote = F)
print(round(rbind(var.t, var.c), 3))
print(cat("\n\n"))
print(cat("Indicator correlation matrix: Taxon", "\n"), quote = F)
print(round(cor.t, 3))
print(avg.offdiag(cor.t))
```

119

```
print(cat("\n"))
print(cat("Indicator correlation matrix: Complement", "\n"), quote = F)
print(round(cor.c, 3))
print(avg.offdiag(cor.c))
print(cat("\n\n"))
print(cat("Observed correlation matrix", "\n"), quote = F)
print(round(obs.cov, 3))
print(avg.offdiag(obs.cov))
print(cat("\n\n"))
print(cat("Predicted correlation matrix", "\n"), quote = F)
print(round(predict.cov, 3))
print(avg.offdiag(predict.cov))
resid.cov <- obs.cov - predict.cov
print(cat("\n\n"))
print(cat("Residual correlation matrix", "\n"), quote = F)
print(round(resid.cov, 3))
print(avg.offdiag(resid.cov)) #

#------compute GFI index and return results as list------#
ipredict <- solve(predict.cov)
eye <- diag(rep(1, nrow(ipredict)))
num1 <- ((ipredict %*% obs.cov) - eye)
num1 <- num1 %*% num1
num <- sum(diag(num1))
den1 <- (ipredict %*% obs.cov)
den1 <- den1 %*% den1
den <- sum(diag(den1))
gfi <- 1 - (num/den)
print(cat("GFI =", gfi, "\n"))
list(mu.t = mu.t, mu.c = mu.c, var.t = var.t, var.c =
var.c, pt.x = pt.x.tilda)
}
```

COMB

DESCRIPTION

Returns all possible indicator combinations for a MAXCOV-HITMAX analysis

USAGE

`COMB(nitems)`

REQUIRED ARGUMENTS

- **nitems**: the number of conjectured taxon indicators; nitems must be ≥4

If the program runs to completion, it produces the following output:

- All possible indicator combinations for a MAXCOV-HITMAX analysis—for example, with 4 indicators, it is possible to conduct 12 quasi-independent MAXCOV analyses:

Combination Number	Indicator Number		
1	1	3	2
2	1	4	2
3	1	4	3
4	2	3	1
5	2	4	1
6	2	4	3
7	3	2	1
8	3	4	1
9	3	4	2
10	4	2	1
11	4	3	1
12	4	3	2

COMB Program Code

```r
COMB<-function(nitems)
{
ans <- matrix(0, ncol = 3, nrow = 1)
print("Thinking very hard")
xnum <- 1:nitems
for(i in 1:length(xnum))
  {
  x <- expand.grid(xnum[-i], xnum[-i], xnum[i])
  xx <- x[x[, 1] != x[, 2] & x[, 1] != x[, 3] & x[, 2] != x[, 3], ]
  x <- t(apply((xx[, 1:2]), 1, sort))
  nvar <- ncol(x)
  n <- seq(ncol(x))
  arglist <- paste("x[, ", n, "]")
  arglist <- paste(arglist, collapse = ", ")
  fcall <- parse(text = paste("table(", arglist, ")"))
  x.table <- eval(fcall)
  x.names <- dimnames(x.table)
  n <- seq(length(x.names))
  arglist <- paste("x.names[[", n, "]]", collapse = ", ")
  fcall <- parse(text = paste("expand.grid(", arglist, ")"))
  x.grid <- eval(fcall)
  x.grid$Counts <- as.vector(x.table)
  new.grid <- (x.grid[x.grid$Counts > 0, ])
  temp <- cbind(new.grid[, 1:2], rep(i, nrow(new.grid)))
  ans <- rbind(ans, as.matrix(temp))
  }
nr <- nrow(ans); nc <- ncol(ans)
ans <- matrix(as.numeric(ans), nrow = nr, ncol = nc)
ans <- ans[2:nr, ]
return(ans[, c(3, 2, 1)])
}
```

Appendix C:
MAXEIG-HITMAX

DESCRIPTION

Returns a MAXEIG plot and an estimate of the taxon base rate; MAXEIG is a multivariate generalization of MAXCOV-HITMAX

USAGE

```
MAXEIG(x, input=1, windows=40, Overlap=.90)
```

REQUIRED ARGUMENTS

- **x**: a matrix of indicator scores
- **input**: column number of matrix **x** that contains the sorting variable
- **windows**: the number of (possibly) sliding windows (x-slabs)
- **Overlap**: percentage overlap between contiguous x-slabs

If the program runs to completion, it produces the following output:

- MAXEIG plot
- An estimate of the taxon base rate and the indicator hitmax threshold score

MAXEIG Program Code

```
function(x, input = 1, windows = 40, make.plot = T,
Overlap=.90, wts = F)
{
#=====================================================================#
# S-Plus code for MAXEIG-HITMAX                                       #
# by Niels G. Waller                                                  #
#                                                                     #
# Program arguments                                                   #
# x= matrix of indicator scores                                      #
# input = MAXEIG sorting variable                                     #
# windows = number of sliding windows for x-slabs                     #
# Overlap = percentage overlap between contiguous x-slabs             #
# wts = T for experimental weighting function                         #
#                                                                     #
#=====================================================================#
#---------------standardize data-------------------#
    x <- apply(x, 2, scale) #
    x <- x[order(x[, input]), ] #
#-----calculate possibly weighted covariances-----------#
    W.Cov <- function(data, weights)
    {
        n <- dim(data)[1]
        center <- rep(1/sum(weights), n) %*% (weights * data))[, ]
        data <- sweep(data, 2, center)
        data <- sqrt(weights) * data
        return((t(data) %*% data)/sum(weights))
    }
#-----create sliding windows on input variable-----#
    make.window <- function(x, number = 40, overlap = 0.9)
    {
        X <- sort(x)
```

```r
if(overlap >= 1) {
    m.per.int <- (length(X) + (number-1) * overlap) /
        number
        m.over <- overlap
}
else {
    m.per.int <- length(X)/(number * (1-overlap) +
        overlap)
    m.over <- overlap * m.per.irt
}
left <- round((0:(number-1)) * (m.per.int-m.over) + 1)
right <- round((1:number) * (m.per.int-m.over) + m.over)
print(cat("The average # of observations in each window = ", trunc(m.per.int), "\n"))
return(cbind(X[left], X[right]))
}

#-----------------------------------------------------------------------------#
    endpoints <- make.window(x[, input], number = windows, overlap =
        Overlap) #
#-----------------------------------------------------------------------------#
    maxroot1 <- numeric(windows)          #------------initialize maxroot1
#-----------------------------------------------------------------------------#
                                          #------compute weighted covariance matrix in window------------#
    for(i in 1:windows) {
        slabdata <- x[(x[, input] >= endpoints[i, 1] & x[, input] <=
            endpoints[i, 2]), ] #
        if(wts == T) {
            weights <- dnorm(scale(1:nrow(slabdata)))^2
        }
        else weights <- rep(1, dim(slabdata)[1]) #
        covmat <- W.Cov(slabdata, weights) #
                                          #------take off diagonal of covmat---------------------------#
        covmat <- covmat-diag(diag(covmat)) #
#======calculate latent roots================================#
```

```
        maxroot1[i] <- eigen(covmat)$values[1]
    }

#====smooth eigenvalues with running medians smoother====#
    smooth1 <- smooth(maxroot1, twice = T)
    smooth1[smooth1 < 0] <- 0#

#------------------------------------------------------------#

#------- x-axis equals midpoints of x-slabs -------#
    xsteps <- (endpoints[, 1] + endpoints[, 2])/2  #
    if(make.plot == T) {
        plot(xsteps, smooth1, axes = F, type = "o", pch = "o", main
            = "MAXEIG", ylab = "Eigenvalues", xlab = "Sliding Windows")
    }

#-------------------------------------------------------------#
# find window max eigenvalue and calculate baserate          #
#-------------------------------------------------------------#
    max.eig <- max(smooth1)
    maxeig.index <- (1:(length(smooth1)))[smooth1 == max.eig]
    maxeig.index <- maxeig.index[1] #
    if(overlap != 0) {
    hitmax <- (endpoints[maxeig.index, 1] + endpoints [maxeig.index, 2])/2
    hitnum <- abs(hitmax-x[, input])
    hitnum <- (1:nrow(x))[hitnum == min(hitnum)]
    taxonp <- (dim(x)[1] - hitnum[1])/dim(x)[1]    ;    }
    if(windows >= 100) {
        hitmax <- endpoints[maxeig.index, 1]
        taxonp <- pnorm(-hitmax)
    }

    print(cat("Estimated base rate for indicator ", input, " = ", round(
        taxonp, digits = 3), "\n"), quote = F)
    print(cat("Estimated Hitmax for indicator ", input, " = ", round(
        hitmax, digits = 3), "\n\n\n"), quote = F) #
#==============================================================#
    list(baserate = taxonp, hitmax = hitmax)
}
```

126

Appendix D: L-Mode

DESCRIPTION

Returns an L-Mode plot and various taxonic parameter estimates; L-mode is a taxometric procedure based on the latent modes of a factor-score density plot

USAGE

```
LMODE(data, m1 = -0.001, m2 = 0.001)
```

REQUIRED ARGUMENTS

- **data**: a matrix of indicator scores
- **m1 & m2:** m1 and m2 are program defaults. Lower mode is highest point on factor-score density below m1, upper mode is highest point on density above m2. One or both of these parameters should be changed when base rate <<.50.

If the program runs to completion, it produces the following output:

- **p.est1**: base rate estimate 1: Eq (5.18)
- **p.est2**: base rate estimate 2: Eq (5.20)
- **p.avg**: average of p.est1 and p.est2
- **baserate**: empirical base rate estimate from taxon membership scores
- **fs$loadings**: factor pattern coefficients
- **tmean1**: indicator mean profile for taxon class: Eq (5.10)
- **cmean1**: indicator mean profile for complement class: Eq (5.11)
- **tmean2**: indicator mean profile for taxon class; empirical estimate
- **cmean2**: indicator mean profile for complement class; empirical estimate

L-Mode Program Code

```
LMODE <- function(data, m1 = -0.001, m2 = 0.001)
{
#==================================================#
#Lmode(x)                                          #
#==================================================#
#
#-calculate means and standard deviations of raw data-#
xmn <- apply(data, 2, mean)
stdev <- function(x)
        {
        sqrt(var(x))
        }
xsd <- apply(data, 2, stdev)
#
#---perform factor analysis on data matrix, compute WLS scores----#
fs <- factanal(data, factors = 1, type = "weighted.ls",iter.max = 50)
#
#----compute density of factor scores, plot scores, find modes-----#
xx <- density(fs$scores)
win.graph()
plot(smooth(xx$x), smooth(xx$y), type = "l", main = "Density of Factor Scores",
     xlim = c(-3.2, 3.2), xlab = "Factor Scores", ylab = "Density") #
maxy1 <- max(smooth(xx$y)[xx$x <= m1])
model.index <- (1:(length(xx$x)))[smooth(xx$y) == maxy1] #
#
if(length(model.index) > 1)
        {
        model.index >- model.index[1]
        }
abline(v = xx$x[model.index])
```

```
maxy2 <- max(smooth(xx$y)[xx$x > m2])
mode2.index <- (1:(length(xx$x)))[smooth(xx$y) == maxy2]    #
#
if(length(mode2.index) > 1)
     {
     mode2.index <- mode2.index[1]
     }
abline(v = xx$x[mode2.index])          #
#
#----compute base rate estimates: Eqs (5.10) & (5.11)-----#
p.est1 <- 1/(1 + xx$x[mode2.index]^2)
p.est2 <- 1 - 1/(1 + xx$x[mode1.index]^2)
pavg <- (p.est1 + p.est2)/2
q <- 1 - pavg #
#
#---------------------------------------------------------#
#calculate indicator class means based on factor loadings  #
#Eqs (5.18) & (5.20)                                        #
#---------------------------------------------------------#
tmean1 <- xmn + xsd * (q/sqrt(pavg * q) * as.vector(fs$loadings)) #
cmean1 <- xmn + xsd * (-pavg/sqrt(pavg * q) * as.vector(fs$loadings)) #
#
#------------------------classify subjects-----------------#
taxon <- matrix(0, length(fs$scores), 1)
dif1 <- abs(fs$scores - xx$x[mode1.index])
dif2 <- abs(fs$scores - xx$x[mode2.index])    #
#
for(i in 1:length(fs$scores))
     {
     if(dif2[i] < dif1[i])
          {
          taxon[i] <- 1
          }
     }
```

```
#-------------------------------------------------------------#
#calculate indicator class means and empirical base rate based on  #
#taxon membership                                              #
#-------------------------------------------------------------#
tmean2 <- apply(data[taxon == 1, ], 2, mean)
cmean2 <- apply(data[taxon == 0, ], 2, mean)
baserate <- sum(taxon)/length(fs$scores)
list(p.est1 = p.est1, p.est2 = p.est2, pavg = pavg,
     baserate = baserate, factor.loadings = fs$loadings,
     tmean1 = tmean1, cmean1 = cmean1,
     tmean2 = tmean2, cmean2 = cmean2)
}
```

131

References

Aiken, L. S., & West, S. G. (1991). *Multiple regression: Testing and interpreting interactions.* Newbury Park, CA: Sage.

Aitken, M., & Rubin, D. B. (1985). Estimation and hypothesis testing in finite mixture models. *Journal of the Royal Statistical Society, Ser. B*(47), 67-75.

American Psychiatric Association. (1994). *Diagnostic and statistical manual of mental disorders: DSM-IV.* Washington, DC: Author.

Aplin, Y. (1987). Classification of dyspraxia in hearing-impaired children using the Q-technique of factor analysis. *Journal of Child Psychology & Psychiatry & Allied Disciplines, 28,* 581-596.

Arffa, S., Fitzhugh-Bell, K., & Black, F. W. (1989). Neuropsychological profiles of children with learning disabilities and children with documented brain damage. *Journal of Learning Disabilities, 22,* 635-640.

Atiya, A. F. (1990). An unsupervised learning technique for artificial neural networks. *Neural Networks, 3,* 707-711.

Bartholomew, D. J. (1987). *Latent variable models and factor analysis.* London: Oxford University Press.

Bartlett, M. S. (1937). The statistical conception of mental factors. *British Journal of Psychology, 28,* 97-104.

Bayes, T. (1763). An essay towards solving a problem in the doctrine of chances. *Philosophical Transactions of the Royal Society, 53,* 370-418.

Bernstein-Carlson, E. B., & Putnam, F. W. (1986). Development, reliability, and validity of a dissociation scale. *Journal of Nervous and Mental Disease, 174,* 727-735.

Blashfield, R. K., & Aldenderfer, M. S. (1988). The methods and problems of cluster analysis. In J. R. Nesselroade & R. B. Cattell (Eds.), *Handbook of multivariate experimental psychology* (2nd ed., pp. 447-473). New York: Plenum.

133

Block, J. (1955). The difference between Q and R. *Psychological Review, 62,* 356-358.
Block, J. (1971). *Lives through time.* Berkeley, CA: Bancroft Books.
Bolles, R. C. (1962). The difference between statistical hypotheses and scientific hypotheses. *Psychological Reports, 11,* 639-645.
Brown, S. R. (1968). Bibliography on Q technique and its methodology. *Perceptual and Motor Skills, 26,* 587-613.
Brush, S. G. (1989). Prediction and theory evaluation: The case of light bending. *Science, 246,* 1124-1129.
Brush, S. G. (1995). Dynamics of theory change: The role of predictions. *PSA 1994 [Proceedings of the Philosophy of Science Association], 2,* 133-145.
Burt, C., & Stephenson, W. (1939). Alternative views on correlations between persons. *Psychometrika, 4,* 269-281.
Burt, C. L. (1912). The mental differences between the sexes. *Journal of Experimental Pedagology, 1,* 273-284.
Burt, C. L. (1917). *The distribution and relations of educational abilities.* London: P. S. King.
Burt, C. L. (1940). *The factors of the mind.* London: University of London Press.
Carnap, R. (1936-1937). Testability and meaning. *Philosophy of Science, 3,* 420-471; *4,* 2-40. Reprinted with corrigenda and additional bibliography, New Haven, CT: Yale University Graduate Philosophy Club, 1950. Reprinted in H. Feigl & M. Broadbeck (Eds.), *Readings in the philosophy of science* (pp. 47-92). New York: Appleton-Century-Crofts, 1953.
Carnap, R. (1962). *Logical foundations of probability* (2nd ed.). Chicago: University of Chicago Press. (Original work published 1950)
Carrier, M. (1991). What is wrong with the miracle argument? *Studies in History and Philosophy of Science, 22,* 23-26.
Cattell, R. B. (1946). *Description and measurement of personality.* New York: World Book.
Cattell, R. B. (1952). The three basic factor analytic research designs—their interrelations and derivatives. *Psychological Bulletin, 49,* 499-520.
Cattell, R. B. (1957). *Personality and motivation structure and measurement.* New York: World Book.
Clogg, C. C., & Shockey, J. W. (1988). Multivariate analysis of discrete data. In J. R. Nesselroade & R. B. Cattell (Eds.), *Handbook of multivariate experimental psychology* (pp. 337-366). New York: Plenum.
Cohen, J. (1968). Multiple regression as a general data-analytic system. *Psychological Bulletin, 70,* 426-443.
Cohen, J. (1992). Fuzzy methodology. *Psychological Bulletin, 112*(3), 409-410.
Cohen, L. M., Berzoff, J. N., & Elin, M. R. (1995). *Dissociative identity disorder: Theoretical and treatment controversies.* Northvale, NJ: Jason Aronson.
Cronbach, L. J., & Gleser, G. C. (1953). Assessing similarity between profiles. *Psychological Bulletin, 50,* 456-473.
Dahlstrom, W. G. (1972). *Personality systematics and the problem of types.* Morristown, NJ: General Learning Press.
Earman, J., & Glymour, C. (1980). Relativity and eclipses: The British eclipse expeditions of 1919 and their predecessors. *Historical Studies in the Physical Sciences, 11,* 49-85.
Erlenmeyer-Kimling, L., Golden, R. R., & Cornblatt, B. A. (1989). A taxometric analysis of cognitive and neuromotor variables in children at risk for schizophrenia. *Journal of Abnormal Psychology, 98,* 203-208.

Everitt, B. S. (1993). *Cluster analysis* (3rd ed.). New York: Halsted.

Eysenck, H. J. (1954). The science of personality: Nomothetic! *Psychological Review, 61,* 339-342.

Fals-Stewart, W., & Lucente, S. (1993). An MCMI cluster typology of obsessive-compulsives: A measure of personality characteristics and its relationship to treatment participation, compliance and outcome in behavior therapy. *Journal of Psychiatric Research, 27,* 139-154.

Faust, D. (1984). *The limits of scientific reasoning.* Minneapolis: University of Minnesota Press.

Faust, D., & Meehl, P. E. (1992). Using scientific methods to resolve enduring questions within the history and philosophy of science: Some illustrations. *Behavior Therapy, 23,* 195-211.

Fleiss, J. L., Lawlor, W., Platman, S. R., & Fieve, R. D. (1971). On the use of inverted factor analysis for generating typologies. *Journal of Abnormal Psychology, 77,* 127-132.

Fowlkes, E. B. (1979). Some methods for studying the mixture of two normal (lognormal) distributions. *Journal of the American Statistical Association, 74,* 561-575.

Freud, S. (1962a). The aetiology of hysteria. In J. Strachey (Ed. & Trans.), *Standard edition of the complete psychological works of Sigmund Freud* (Vol. 3, pp. 191-221). London: Hogarth. (Original work published 1896)

Freud, S. (1962b). Further remarks on the neuro-psychoses of defence. In J. Strachey (Ed. & Trans.), *Standard edition of the complete psychological works of Sigmund Freud* (Vol. 3, pp. 162-185). London: Hogarth. (Original work published 1896)

Freud, S. (1962c). Heredity and the aetiology of the neuroses. In J. Strachey (Ed. & Trans.), *Standard edition of the complete psychological works of Sigmund Freud* (Vol. 3, pp. 143-156). London: Hogarth. (Original work published 1896)

Gibson, W. A. (1959). Three multivariate models: Factor analysis, latent structure analysis, and latent profile analysis. *Psychometrika, 24,* 229-252.

Golden, R. R. (1982). A taxometric model for the detection of a conjectured latent taxon. *Multivariate Behavioral Research, 17,* 389-416.

Golden, R. R. (1991). Bootstrapping taxometrics: On the development of a method for detection of a single major gene. In W. M. Grove & D. Cicchetti (Eds.), *Thinking clearly about psychology: Vol. 2. Personality and psychopathology* (pp. 259-294). Minneapolis: University of Minnesota Press.

Golden, R. R., Vaughan, H. G., Jr., Kurtzberg, D., & McCarton, C. M. (1988). Detection of neonatal brain dysfunction without the use of a criterion variable: Analysis of the statistical problem with an illustrative example. In P. Vietze & H. G. Vaughan, Jr. (Eds.), *Early identification of infants at risk for mental retardation* (pp. 71-95). Orlando, FL: Grune & Stratton.

Gorsuch, R. L. (1983). *Factor analysis* (2nd ed.). Hillsdale, NJ: Lawrence Erlbaum.

Graybill, F. A. (1983). *Matrices with applications in statistics* (2nd ed.). Belmont, CA: Wadsworth.

Grayson, D. A. (1987). Can categorical and dimensional views of psychiatric illness be distinguished? *British Journal of Psychiatry, 151,* 355-361.

Green, P. E. (1978). *Analyzing multivariate data.* Hinsdale, IL: Dryden.

Grove, W. M., & Meehl, P. E. (1993). Simple regression-based procedures for taxometric investigations. *Psychological Reports, 73,* 707-737.

Haertel, E. H. (1990). Continuous and discrete latent structure models for item response data. *Psychometrika, 55,* 477-494.

136   MULTIVARIATE TAXOMETRIC PROCEDURES

Harman, H. H. (1976). *Modern factor analysis.* Chicago: University of Chicago Press.
Harris, G. T., Rice, M. E., & Quinsey, V. L. (1994). Psychopathy as a taxon: Evidence that psychopaths are a discrete class. *Journal of Consulting and Clinical Psychology, 62,* 387-397.
Haslam, N., & Beck, A. T. (1993). Categorization of major depression in an outpatient sample. *Journal of Nervous and Mental Disease, 181,* 725-731.
Highfield, R., & Carter, P. (1994). *The private lives of Albert Einstein.* New York: St. Martin's.
Howson, C., & Urbach, P. (1993). *Scientific reasoning: The Bayesian approach.* Chicago, IL: Open Court.
Hull, D. L. (1988). *Science as a process.* Chicago: University of Chicago Press.
Imbrie, J., & Purdy, E. (1962). Classification of modern Bahamian carbonate sediments. *American Association of Petroleum Geologists: Memoir, 7,* 253-272.
Jackson, J. E. (1991). *A user's guide to principal components.* New York: John Wiley.
Janet, P. (1889). *L'Automatisme psychologique.* Paris: Felix Alcan.
Jöreskog, K. G., & Sörbom, D. (1988). *LISREL 7: A guide to the program and applications.* Chicago: SPSS.
Keynes, J. M. (1929). *A treatise on probability.* New York: Macmillan.
Kim, J.-O., & Mueller, C. W. (1978). *An introduction to factor analysis. What it is and how to do it* (Sage University Paper series on Quantitative Applications in the Social Sciences, No. 07-013). Beverly Hills, CA: Sage.
Kohonen, T. (1995). *Self-organizing maps.* Berlin: Springer.
Korfine, L., & Lenzenweger, M. F. (1995). The taxonicity of schizotypy: A replication. *Journal of Abnormal Psychology, 104,* 26-31.
Kries, J. von. (1886). *Die Principen der Wahrscheinlichkeitsrechnung: Eine logische Untersuchung.* Freiburg, Germany: Mohr.
Kuhn, T. (1962). *The structure of scientific revolutions.* Chicago: University of Chicago Press.
Langeheine, R., & Rost, J. (Eds.). (1988). *Latent trait and latent class models.* New York: Plenum.
Lazarsfeld, P. F., & Henry, N. W. (1968). *Latent structure analysis.* Boston: Houghton Mifflin.
Lenzenweger, M. F., & Korfine, L. (1992). Confirming the latent structure and base rate of schizotypy: A taxometric analysis. *Journal of Abnormal Psychology, 101,* 567-571.
Lindsay, B. G., & Basak, P. (1993). Multivariate normal mixtures: A fast consistent method of moments. *Journal of the American Statistical Association, 88,* 468-476.
Lowrie, G. S., & Raulin, M. L. (1990, March-April). *Search for schizophrenia and nonschizophrenic taxonomies in a college population.* Paper presented at the 61st annual convention of the Eastern Psychological Association, Philadelphia.
Lykken, D. T. (1991). What's wrong with psychology anyway? In D. Cicchetti & W. M. Grove (Eds.), *Thinking clearly about psychology: Vol. 1. Matters of public interest* (pp. 3-39). Minneapolis: University of Minnesota Press.
Lynn, S. J., & Rhue, J. W. (Eds.). (1994). *Dissociation: Clinical and theoretical perspectives.* New York: Guilford.
Mayo, D. G. (1996). *Error and the growth of experimental knowledge.* Chicago: University of Chicago Press.
McDonald, R. P. (1962). A general approach to nonlinear factor analysis. *Psychometrika, 27,* 397-415.
McLachlan, G. J., & Basford, K. E. (1988). *Mixture models: Inference and applications to clustering.* New York: Marcel Dekker.

Meehl, P. E. (1965). *Detecting latent clinical taxa by fallible quantitative indicators lacking an accepted criterion* (Rep. No. PR-65-2). Minneapolis: University of Minnesota, Research Laboratories of the Department of Psychiatry.

Meehl, P. E. (1968). *Detecting latent clinical taxa, II: A simplified procedure, some additional hitmax cut locations, a single-indicator method, and miscellaneous theorems* (Rep. No. PR-68-2). Minneapolis: University of Minnesota, Research Laboratory of the Department of Psychiatry.

Meehl, P. E. (1972). Specific genetic etiology, psychodynamics and therapeutic nihilism. *International Journal of Mental Health, 1,* 10-27. Reprinted in P. E. Meehl, *Psychodiagnosis: Selected papers* (pp. 182-199). Minneapolis: University of Minnesota Press, 1973.

Meehl, P. E. (1973a). MAXCOV-HITMAX: A taxonomic search method for loose genetic syndromes. In P. E. Meehl, *Psychodiagnosis: Selected papers* (pp. 200-224). Minneapolis: University of Minnesota Press.

Meehl, P. E. (1973b). Why I do not attend case conferences. In P. E. Meehl, *Psychodiagnosis: Selected papers* (pp. 225-302). Minneapolis: University of Minnesota Press.

Meehl, P. E. (1977). Specific etiology and other forms of strong influence: Some quantitative meanings. *Journal of Medicine and Philosophy, 2,* 33-53.

Meehl, P. E. (1978). Theoretical risks and tabular asterisks: Sir Karl, Sir Ronald, and the slow progress of soft psychology. *Journal of Consulting and Clinical Psychology, 46,* 806-834.

Meehl, P. E. (1983). Subjectivity in psychoanalytic inference: The nagging persistence of Willhelm Fleiss's Achensee question. In J. Earman (Ed.), *Minnesota studies in the philosophy of science: Vol. 10. Testing scientific theories* (pp. 349-411). Minneapolis: University of Minnesota Press.

Meehl, P. E. (1986). Diagnostic taxa as open concepts: Metatheoretical and statistical questions about reliability and construct validity in the grand strategy of nosological revision. In T. Millon & G. L. Klerman (Eds.), *Contemporary directions in psychopathology* (pp. 215-231). New York: Guilford.

Meehl, P. E. (1990a). Appraising and amending theories: The strategy of Lakatosian defense and two principles that warrant using it. *Psychological Inquiry, 1,* 108-141, 173-180.

Meehl, P. E. (1990b). *Corroboration and verisimilitude: Against Lakatos' "sheer leap of faith"* (Working paper, No. MCPS-90-01). Minneapolis: University of Minnesota Center for the Philosophy of Science.

Meehl, P. E. (1990c). Schizotaxia as an open concept. In A. I. Rabin, R. Zucker, R. Emmons, & S. Frank (Eds.), *Studying persons and lives* (pp. 248-303). New York: Springer.

Meehl, P. E. (1990d). Toward an integrated theory of schizotaxia, schizotypy, and schizophrenia. *Journal of Personality Disorders, 4,* 1-99.

Meehl, P. E. (1990e). Why summaries of research on psychological theories are often uninterpretable. *Psychological Reports, 66,* 195-244. Reprinted in R. E. Snow & D. Wiley (Eds.), *Improving inquiry in social science: A volume in honor of Lee J. Cronbach* (pp. 13-59). Hillsdale, NJ: Lawrence Erlbaum, 1991.

Meehl, P. E. (1992a). Cliometric metatheory; The actuarial approach to empirical, history-based philosophy of science. *Psychological Reports, 71,* 339-467.

Meehl, P. E. (1992b). Factors and taxa, traits and types, differences of degree and differences in kind. *Journal of Personality, 60,* 117-174.

Meehl, P. E. (1992c). The miracle argument for realism: An important lesson to be learned by generalizing from Carrier's counter-examples. *Studies in History and Philosophy of Science, 23,* 267-282.

Meehl, P. E. (1995a). Bootstraps taxometrics: Solving the classification problem in psychopathology. *American Psychologist, 50,* 266-275.

Meehl, P. E. (1995b). Extension of the MAXCOV-HITMAX taxometric procedure to situations of sizable nuisance covariance. In D. Lubinski & R. Dawis (Eds.), *Assessing individual differences in human behavior: New concepts, methods, and findings* (pp. 81-92). Palo Alto, CA: Consulting Psychologists Press.

Meehl, P. E. (1997). The problem is epistemology, not statistics: Replace significance tests by confidence intervals and quantify accuracy of risky numerical predictions. In L. L. Harlow, S. A. Mulaik, & J. H. Steiger (Eds.), *What if there were no significance tests?* (pp. 393-425). Mahwah, NJ: Lawrence Erlbaum.

Meehl, P. E., & Golden, R. R. (1982). Taxometric methods. In P. Kendall & J. Butcher (Eds.), *Handbook of research methods in clinical psychology* (pp. 127-181). New York: John Wiley.

Meehl, P. E., & Yonce, L. J. (1994). Taxometric analysis: I. Detecting taxonicity with two quantitative indicators using means above and means below a sliding cut (MAMBAC procedure). *Psychological Reports, 74,* 1059-1274.

Meehl, P. E., & Yonce, L. J. (1996). Taxometric analysis: II. Detecting taxonicity using covariance of two quantitative indicators in successive intervals of a third indicator (MAXCOV procedure). *Psychological Reports, Monograph Supplement, 1-V78,* 1091-1227.

Mill, J. S. (1843). *A system of logic.* London: Longmans, Green.

Molenaar, P. C., & Von Eye, A. (1994). On the arbitrary nature of latent variables. In A. Von Eye & C. Clogg (Eds.), *Latent variable analysis* (pp. 227-242). Thousand Oaks, CA: Sage.

Moss, W. W. (1983). Taxa, taxonomists, and taxonomy. In J. Felsenstein (Ed.), *Numerical taxonomy* (pp. 72-75). New York: Springer-Verlag.

Murphy, E. A. (1964). One cause? Many causes? The argument from the bimodal distribution. *Journal of Chronic Disease, 17,* 301-324.

Murtagh, F. (1995). Interpreting the Kohonen self-organizing feature map using contiguity-constrained clustering. *Pattern Recognition Letters, 16,* 399-408.

North, C. S., Ryall, J. M., Ricci, D. A., & Wetzel, R. D. (1993). *Multiple personalities, multiple disorders: Psychiatric classification and media influence.* Oxford: Oxford University Press.

Nunnally, J. (1962). The analysis of profile data. *Psychological Bulletin, 59,* 311-319.

Osgood, C. E., & Suci, G. J. (1952). A measure of relation determined by both mean differences and profile information. *Psychological Bulletin, 49,* 251-262.

Pais, A. (1991). *Niels Bohr's times, in physics, philosophy, and polity.* New York: Oxford University Press.

Pap, A. (1953). Reduction-sentences and open concepts. *Methodos, 5,* 3-30.

Pap, A. (1958). *Semantics and necessary truth.* New Haven, CT: Yale University Press.

Pearson, K. (1895). Contributions to the mathematical theory of evolution, V: Skew variation in homogeneous material. *Philosophical Transactions, Ser. A. 186,* 342-414.

Popper, K. R. (1959). *The logic of scientific discovery.* New York: Basic Books. (Original work published 1934)

Popper, K. R. (1962). *Conjectures and refutations.* New York: Basic Books.

Popper, K. R. (1983). *Postscript (Vol. 1): Realism and the aim of science.* Totowa, NJ: Rowman & Littlefield.

Robertson, C. A., & Fryer, J. G. (1969). Some descriptive properties of normal mixtures. *Skandinavian Aktuarietidskrift, 52,* 137-146.

Robins, R. W., John, O. P., Caspi, A., Moffit, T. E., & Stouthamer-Loeber, M. (1996). Resilient, overcontrolled, and undercontrolled boys: Three replicable personality types. *Journal of Personality and Social Psychology, 70,* 157-171.

Roeder, K. (1994). A graphical technique for determining the number of components in a mixture of normals. *Journal of the American Statistical Association, 89,* 487-495.

Rost, J. (1990). Rasch models in latent classes: An integration of two approaches to item analysis. *Applied Psychological Measurement, 14,* 271-282.

Rost, J. (1991). A logistic mixture distribution model for polychotomous item responses. *British Journal of Mathematical and Statistical Psychology, 44,* 75-92.

Salmon, W. C. (1973). Confirmation. *Scientific American, 228,* 75-83.

Salmon, W. C. (1984). *Scientific explanation and the causal structure of the world.* Princeton, NJ: Princeton University Press.

Scherr, G. H. (Ed.). (1983). Irreproducible science: Editor's introduction. In *The Best of the Journal of Irreproducible Results.* New York: Workman.

Silverman, B. W. (1986). *Density estimation for statistics and data analysis.* London: Chapman & Hall.

Sokal, R., & Michener, C. D. (1958). A statistical method for evaluating systematic relationships. *University of Kansas Scientific Bulletin, 38,* 1409-1438.

StatSci. (1993). *S-Plus for Windows user's manual.* (Available from Statistical Sciences, Inc., 1700 Westlake Avenue N., Suite 500, Seattle, WA 98109)

Stephenson, W. (1935). Correlating persons instead of tests. *Character and Personality, 4,* 211-216.

Stephenson, W. (1936a). The foundations of psychometry: Four factor systems. *Psychometrika, 1,* 195-209.

Stephenson, W. (1936b). Introduction of inverted factor analysis with some applications to studies of orexia. *Journal of Educational Psychology, 5,* 353-367.

Stephenson, W. (1952). Some observations on Q technique. *Psychological Bulletin, 49,* 483-498.

Strube, M. J. (1989). Evidence for the type in Type A behavior: A taxometric analysis. *Journal of Personality and Social Psychology, 56,* 972-987.

Takane, Y. (1976). A statistical procedure for the latent profile model. *Japanese Psychological Research, 18,* 82-90.

Tanaka, J. S., & Huba, G. J. (1989). A general coefficient of determination for covariance structure models under arbitrary GLS estimation. *British Journal of Mathematical and Statistical Psychology, 42,* 233-239.

Thurstone, L. L. (1935). *The vectors of mind.* Chicago: University of Chicago Press.

Thurstone, L. L. (1937). Current misuse of the factorial methods. *Psychometrika, 2,* 73-76.

Thurstone, L. L. (1947). *Multiple factor analysis.* Chicago: University of Chicago Press.

Titterington, D. M., Smith, A. F. M., & Makov, U. E. (1985). *Statistical analysis of finite mixture distributions.* New York: John Wiley.

Trull, T. J., Widiger, T. A., & Guthrie, P. (1990). Categorical versus dimensional status of borderline personality disorder. *Journal of Abnormal Psychology, 99,* 40-48.

Tucker, L. R. (1971). Relation of factor score estimates to their use. *Psychometrika, 36,* 427-436.

Tukey, J. W. (1977). *Exploratory data analysis.* Reading, MA: Addison-Wesley.

U.S. Department of Labor, Employment and Training Administration, Employment Service. (1977). *Dictionary of occupational titles* (4th ed.). Washington, DC: Government Printing Office.

Waller, N. G., Kaiser, H. A., Illian, J. B., & Manry, M. (in press). A comparison of the classification capabilities of the 1-dimensional Kohonen Neural Network with two partitioning and three hierarchical cluster analysis algorithms. *Psychometrika.*

Waller, N. G., Putnam, F. W., & Carlson, E. (1996). Types of dissociation and dissociative types: A taxometric analysis of the Dissociative Experiences Scale. *Psychological Methods, 3,* 300-321.

Waller, N. G., & Shaver, P. (1994). The cultural transmission of romantic love styles: A Twin-family study. *Psychological Science, 5,* 268-274.

Waller, N. G., Tellegen, A., McDonald, R. P., & Lykken, D. T. (1996). Exploring nonlinear models in personality assessment: Development and preliminary validation of a negative emotionality scale. *Journal of Personality, 64,* 545-576.

Ward, J. H. (1963). Hierarchical grouping to optimize an objective function. *Journal of the American Statistical Association, 58,* 236-244.

Wegman, E. J. (1972). Nonparametric probability density estimation. *Technometrics, 14,* 533-546.

Williams, L. M. (1994). The multidimensional nature of schizotypal traits: A cluster analytic study. *Personality Individual Differences, 16*(1), 103-112.

Worrall, J. (1982). The pressure of light: The strange case of the vacillating "crucial experiment." *Studies in the History and Philosophy of Science, 13,* 133-171.

York, K. L., & John, O. P. (1992). The four faces of Eve: A typological analysis of women's personality at midlife. *Journal of Personality and Social Psychology, 63,* 494-508.

Author Index

Subject Index

Average linkage, 48, 60, 70
 L-Mode, comparison of parameter
  recovery, 69-70

Base rate, 7, 12-17, 20-27, 40-42, 45,
  51-52, 54, 56-60, 67-68, 70-71, 76,
  78-79, 99-101
 and the General Covariance Mixture
  Theorem, 12
 detecting low base rate taxa, 45
 estimation by using:
  L-Mode, 57-59
  MAXCOV, 23-24
 influence on correlations in mixture
  distributions, 14
 influence on typological factor scores,
  51-52
Bayes' Theorem, 7, 100
 origin of, 27
 taxon membership probabilities,
  relationship to, 29
Bimodality, 7, 8, 13, 32, 72
 L-Mode factor score density plots, 72

mixtures, relationship to, 8
not required for taxonicity, 7

Causal Origin Taxa, 5
Cluster analysis, 1, 6, 60, 67, 76
 Average Linkage, 48, 60, 70
 WardÆs Method, 48, 60, 68, 70
Coherent Cut Kinetics, 16, 31, 96
COMB, 29
Commonsense Taxa, 4
Consistency Tests, 25-27
 inchworm consistency test, 45
 L-Mode, built into 58-60
 MAXCOV, when conducting, 25
 model corroboration, role in, 92, 96,
  100-102
Corroboration, 7, 25, 95-96, 102
Crud factor, 17

Dimensions, 2, 5-6, 9, 19, 21-22, 27, 29,
 30, 45, 48, 52-53, 57, 67, 74
Dissociative Identity Disorder, 2, 5, 41,
 74-75, 84, 89

About the Authors

Niels G. Waller is currently Associate Professor of Psychology at the University of California, Davis. He holds a Bachelor of Music in classical guitar performance from the New England Conservatory of Music (1982), a Master of Liberal Arts from Harvard University (1989), and a Ph.D. in clinical psychology and psychometric methods from the University of Minnesota (1990). He has received numerous honors for his work on personality theory, psychometrics, and quantitative genetics, including the Thomas Small prize from Harvard University (1989), the Raymond Cattell award from the Society of Multivariate Experimental Psychology (1997), and the Morton Prince award from the International Society for the Study of Dissociation (1997). He is currently Associate Editor of the *Journal of Personality.*

Paul E. Meehl, a clinical psychologist, received his Ph.D. in 1945 from the University of Minnesota. He is Regents' Professor of Psychology, Emeritus, and Member, Emeritus, of the Minnesota Center for Philosophy of Science at the University of Minnesota. He has done research in animal learning, psychometrics, interview assessment, clinical prediction, and forensic psychology. He is a past president of the American Psychological Association and has received numerous honors, including the APA's Award for Outstanding Lifetime Contribution to Psychology, the APA Clinical

Division's Distinguished Contributor Award and its 1996 Centennial Award, the Bruno Klopfer Award in Personality Assessment, the American Psychological Foundation's Gold Medal Award for Life Achievement in the Application of Psychology, the Society for Research in Psychopathology's Joseph P. Zubin Award for Distinguished Contributions in Psychopathology, and the Educational Testing Service's Award for Distinguished Service to Measurement. He is a Member of the National Academy of Sciences and a Fellow of the American Academy of Arts and Sciences. His books include *Clinical Versus Statistical Prediction* (1954), *Psychodiagnosis* (1973), and *Selected Philosophical and Methodological Papers* (1991). His current work is developing new statistical procedures (taxometric analysis) for classification and genetics of psychopathology, the elaboration of his widely recognized theory of schizophrenia, and formulating psychometric approaches to empirical, history-based philosophy of science.